GIBRALTAR

ROCK OF AGES

Hubert Caetano

This book was first published in Great Britain by
Gibraltar Books Ltd
Gibraltar

A catalogue record of this book is available from the British Library

ISBN 1 919657 07 X

Cover design: Silke Bernau

Typeset by Priory Publications, Horley, Surrey.
Printed in the UK by FotoDirect Ltd.

To

IRIS

By the same author

Angling in the Strait of Gibraltar

About the author

Hubert Caetano was the angling correspondent of the *Gibraltar Chronicle* for many years. Born in 1935, he has lived through the traumatic evacuations of the Second World War and the subsequent troubles with Spain. He was educated at the Gibraltar Grammar School. After retiring from the Civil Service in 1990, he wrote a book on angling in the Strait. Over the last few years, he has also contributed a number of short stories to the *Gibraltar Chronicle.*

Acknowledgement

I would like to thank all the members of my family for their encouragement and many readings and checking of the stories. Particular thanks to Silke for her estimable scrutiny and help and also to Nikki for her succinct and valuable suggestions.

Hubert Caetano

Contents

Foreword

It is no mean task for the author to stretch his literary imagination and historical overview, across the ages from those timeless tectonic upheavals which gave birth to this Rock of Ages washed by the great seas around it, to the equally timeless futuristic outreaches almost eternally distant from us. Hubert Caetano has managed to combine imagination and realism spanning these millennia. At all times he is faithful to the scientific, cultural and historical context in which he places his fascinating stories.

In the 'Last of the Cavemen' the author draws on the latest archaeological evidence pointing to the demise of the Neanderthals. In 'Los Conversos (1474)', 'The Corsairs (1540)' and 'The King's Coach (1624)' he colourfully and often amusingly captures the mediaeval turbulence in a small town (La Villa Vieja and La Barcina) living under the cloud of the Inquisition, the threat of piracy and the ruthlessness of monarchs, dukes and governors.

And moving into times more familiar to us, he describes the horrors of the Spanish Civil War, the war-time tensions pressing upon the loyal people of Gibraltar during World War II, and the traumatic but formative experiences of the Evacuation and Franco's closure of the frontier ('The Last Siege 1965').

A particular innovative feature of this book is the bold attempt to look into the future. The challenge here is to avoid mere 'science fiction' and yet entice the reader into the unknown but potentially viable world still to come. The author here travels along the road of intriguing historical conjecture, for example, 'Operación Calpe 2015 AD'. How plausible are the events related here? It is certainly an unnerving question.

This book is a welcome and valuable addition to the extensive literary stock of what be termed 'Gibraltariana'. It is a pleasure for me through this Foreword to introduce this elegant and very readable book to prospective readers who, I am sure, will enjoy it as much as I have.

Dr B. Linares
Minister for Education and Culture
Gibraltar, January 2003

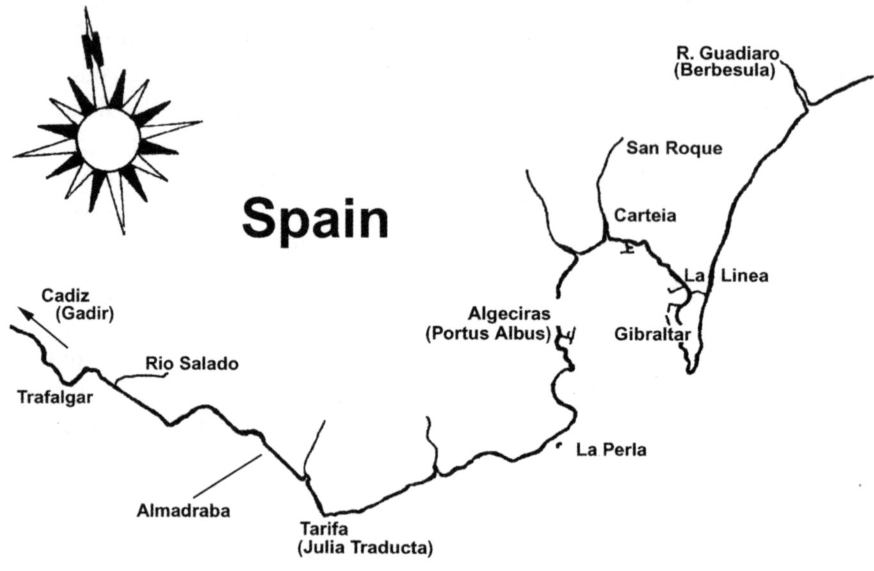

Strait of Gibraltar

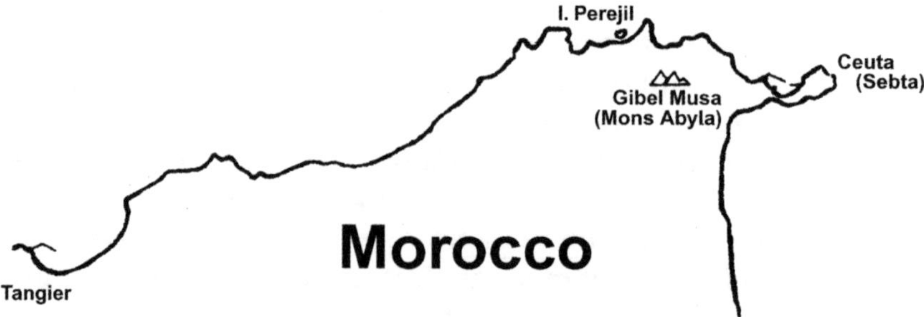

Preface

This book is about the Rock of Gibraltar and its long and varied history, from its creation to the distant future, its settlers, conquerors, the vanquished and those who sought refuge here. It is an attempt to popularise the fascinating history of this great Rock, to embellish the many stark events that have or may have occurred here through the ages with adventure, wonder and romance as experienced by those who lived through these times and thus make its history more personal and therefore more attractive and interesting to the reader. Also to try and look forward to what can or may happen in the future and give this future an aura of drama and excitement.

It consists of short stories from some of the major epochs. Many, like 'The Vandals' and 'The Hermit' are highly imaginative. Others, such as 'Los Conversos' and 'The King's Coach', are based on historical episodes that need little embellishment, whilst a few, like 'Shipwreck', are true stories. In 'Of Kings and Sieges' I have chosen a short section of the Rock's history to show that there has always been trouble of one sort or another in these strategic narrows. Long periods of peace have been comparatively rare, indeed problems continue to this very day, albeit of a less violent nature. Many of the stories are traumatic, even brutal; particularly those of the earlier years, but then most momentous incidents in history tend to be thus. 'Homecoming' which I experienced myself, is mostly factual. I have included it because I believe that the Evacuation in 1940, as well as the later closure of the Frontier, was critical in the final formation of the present Gibraltarian nationality.

The Rock's creation is based on current geological theories whilst other episodes are stories based wholly or partially on pre-historical or historical evidence. In some cases different versions of events exist and I have endeavoured to use the most likely. The future as depicted here may or may not occur, but follows trends which I believe make it plausible. As for the finale, it is of course purely fictional, but well within the bounds of possibility, even if the ultimate causes may turn out to be quite different.

In other words, although I may have used my imagination here and there, everything here did happen, may have happened or may possibly happen.

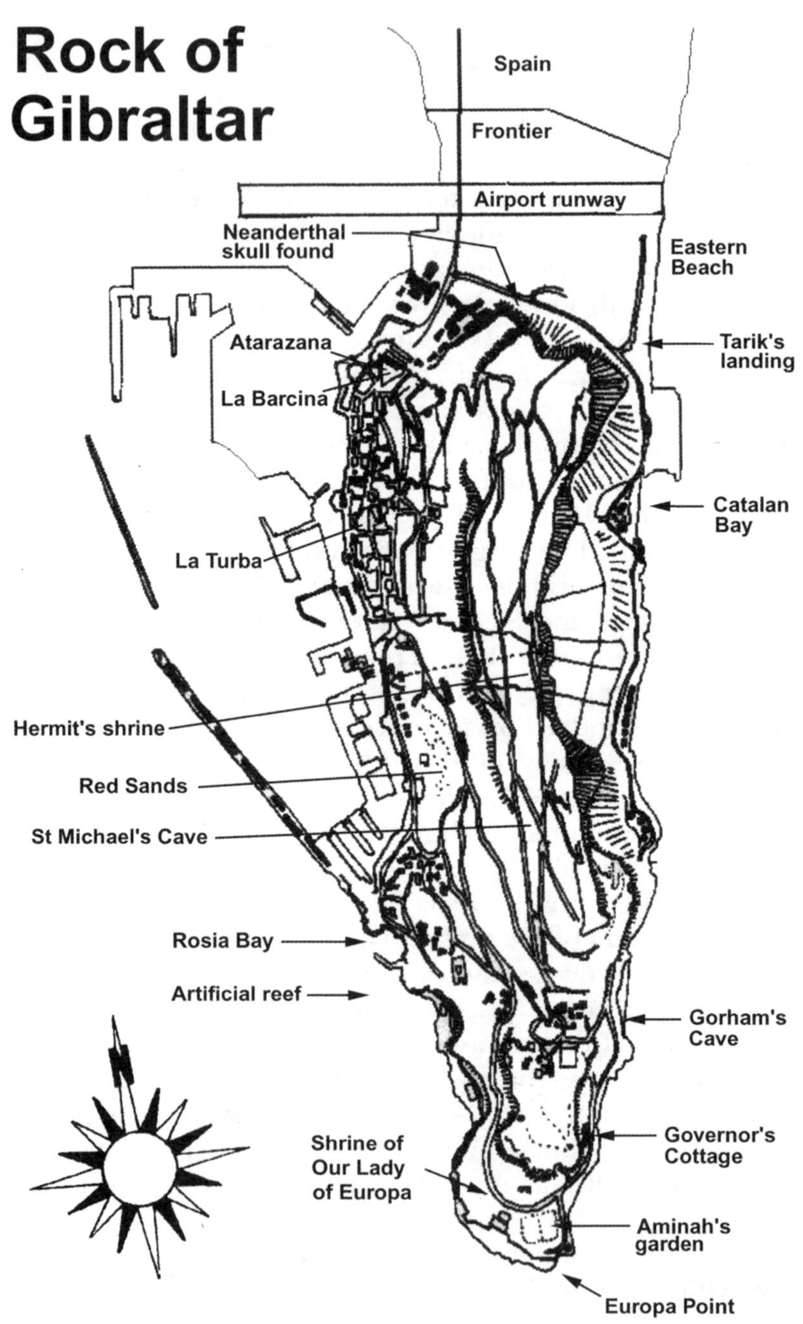
Rock of Gibraltar
Spain
Frontier
Airport runway
Neanderthal skull found
Eastern Beach
Atarazana
Tarik's landing
La Barcina
Catalan Bay
La Turba
Hermit's shrine
Red Sands
St Michael's Cave
Rosia Bay
Artificial reef
Gorham's Cave
Shrine of Our Lady of Europa
Governor's Cottage
Aminah's garden
Europa Point

Introduction

Few can fail to be impressed on first sighting the Rock of Gibraltar. From the east, as the land funnels inwards towards the Strait which bears its name, the two pillars rise majestically on either side of the narrows, guardians of the entrance, and it is easy to visualise why the ancients feared what lay beyond. From the west, as you sail through the Strait and are expecting the blue Mediterranean to open out before you, the Rock juts out as if detached from the coast, like a crouched lion ready to pounce on anyone entering. Even from the air it looks magnificent. It is undoubtedly one of the great geographical and historic sites in the world, famous throughout the ages. It owes this to its strategic position at the entrance to the Mediterranean, cradle of many civilisations, and also as a stepping-stone between two great continents. When the centres of world leadership moved to the North Atlantic, it served as a pivot between these and the older nations within the Mediterranean. Not surprisingly it is known as the key to this sea, the Roman sea, their Mare Nostrum.

Since its possible cataclysmic birth it has undergone many changes. The earth has trembled, the sea levels fluctuated and over the millennia the resulting drastic changes in the weather have eroded it relentlessly. As an offshore island or as a rocky peninsula, situated at the base of a large continent and riddled with caves and cliffs, it has often offered refuge to many species, animals and plants, driven southwards as recurrent ice ages crept over the continent. It is now suspected to have been one of the last refuges of the Neanderthals, maybe as they retreated in front of the increasingly harsh winters and the new wave of more adaptable hominids, the Homo sapiens. After this, when the early civilisations at the other end of the Mediterranean started to expand, its unique and imposing position caused it to be viewed as a dividing line between the real and the nether world, until finally some dared to sail through the narrow Strait. Much later it was the key to the invasion of Europe from North Africa. Constantly fought over, it became a famous fortress controlling the Strait and a synonym for great strength – 'As strong as the Rock of Gibraltar'. Today it remains a bone of contention between Spain, claiming to restore its national integrity, Britain, endeavouring to divest itself of the uncomfortable remnants of empire, and a native people striving desperately to establish their inalienable right to their own land. What of the future? Maybe, as Europe unites and internal nationalisms fade, it will become just another seaport of the new mega-nation. It may even regain its fortress importance of old, guarding the narrow Strait into the Mediterranean Sea, the first bastion of a united Europe, on the frontier dividing it from the African countries to the south.

After that, who knows?

Home thoughts from the sea

'Nobly, nobly Cape Saint Vincent to the North-west died away
Sunset ran, one glorious blood red, reeking into Cadiz Bay
Bluish 'mid the burning water, full in face Trafalgar lay
In the dimmest North-east distance dawned Gibraltar grand and gray.'

Robert Browning

Creation

1

65,000,000 ??

The massive tectonic plate which is destined to become Africa and South America finally splits and the two sections drift away from each other. The African plate moves inexorably northwards towards that other great landmass, the Eurasian. Here it slowly squeezes onto the two shallow seas which eventually coalesce to form the Mediterranean. At the western end, it practically closes one of these from the new Atlantic Ocean. On the bottom of the narrow neck of water that is left lies a thick bed of limestone, a white rock formed and reformed from the compressed calcite remains of millions upon millions of tiny animals that lived and died in similar shallow seas over the aeons.

As the two giant plates come together, this slab is crushed and buckles inwards, its ends tilting upwards, the tips rising above the seas and surrounding landscape, great white peaks rearing up on either side of the shelf of rock thus formed.

There has been much more tilting, crushing and erosion over time, but what remains today of these mounts was known to the ancients as the Pillars of Hercules. The Strait itself, the Fretum Herculeum of the Roman world, was their 'Non Plus Ultra' – there is nothing beyond, for on the horizon of that huge ocean they believed lay the edge of the world. Earlier, these myths had not deterred those great navigators, the Phoenicians, and they had been further promulgated by these canny merchants to keep others from their rich new trading posts on the shores of the great ocean. Belief in this distant horizon as the edge of the world persisted until the fifteenth century.

After the fall of Phoenician port of Tyre to the Assyrians at the other end of the Mediterranean, it was their satellite colony on the North African coast, Carthage, that took over all of these lucrative trading posts on the Iberian mainland. Later, after the Punic wars, the victorious Romans ousted the Carthaginians from the land which they named Hispania. In order to make the government of the large peninsula easier, they divided it into sections and called this rich southern land Baetica. The two Pillars of Hercules at the Strait they called Mons Abyla and Mons Calpe. This latter name apparently derived from the Phoenician word for hollow stone, presumably because of the many caverns visible as one sails along the eastern coastline of the Rock. With the dissolution of the Roman Empire, the area was overrun by bands of barbarian tribes. It was across this Strait that the Vandals, one of the fiercest of these tribes, after devastating Spain, were ousted from this land by yet another wave of barbarians, the Goths, and sailed to Africa. There they finally established their kingdom under their victorious leader Genseric and even ended up sacking Rome itself. Two hundred years later, when the Arabs burst out of Arabia after the death of the Prophet, and in that spectacular wave of conquests arrived here and crossed the Strait, they named the Pillars Gibel Musa and Gibel Tarik, the mountains of Musa and Tarik, after two of the great generals of the Moorish conquests of these lands. Today it is these latter names that have persisted. The pillar to the south on the African coast, the Roman Abyla, is still called Gibel Musa; the one to the north, on the European coastline, is of course Gibraltar, a name derived from the Moorish Gibel Tarik.

For many thousands of years, these imposing pillars have stood guard at these gates; sometimes with a broad valley between them with hardly any water, leading down into the shallow sea beyond and surrounded by vast swathes of jungles or savannahs or even deserts. At others, as islands almost submerged by raging seas with only their topmost peaks signalling the entrance to the narrow Strait opening out onto the great ocean.

Last of the Cavemen

2

circa 30,000 ??

With pounding heart he crouched on the rocky ledge, terrified and exhausted. Far behind he could hear the shrill cries of those creatures, the pale ones. He knew there would be no getting away from them this time, he was the only one left to hunt. From here, practically at the very top of the Rock, he could see all the lands where his ancestors had hunted and even the lake at the centre of the marshy ground and he realised that he was almost directly above the cave where he had been born. A flood of boyhood memories overcame him. He remembered vividly that day, the one of his greatest triumph. It all seemed so long ago.

Our people dwelt in the many caves of this great white mountain. The cavern in which my family lived at the foot of the mount opened out on to a large plain where the men did most of their hunting. When I was still quite young, I discovered a crack in the roof of the cave through which I could just squeeze. Climbing up this, I eventually found myself far above the cave entrance, peering out on to the green sandy plains beyond the trees. I was the only one of the young that dared climb up there. From this, my very own lookout, I would call out to the elders when I saw any game near the lake which, although far away, was clearly visible from this vantage-point. I remember the feeling of importance this gave me.

It was during the time of the cold weather, when there was no game. The men would return each night tired, almost freezing and invariably empty-handed. We were all starving. Indeed, some of the very young, their bellies distended from having been fed on almost inedible roots, had already died. Exhausted and hungry, I would crawl slowly up the crack every morning and scan the surrounding landscape hopefully, but there was nothing, just snow and ice everywhere. Then, early one morning, just after the men had left, I saw it, a monster animal such as I had never seen before. It came lumbering out of the frozen trees to the lakeshore. I climbed quickly down to tell the women and they listened excitedly, until, that is, I described the beast – a giant on five legs and brandishing two long white horns. Then they just laughed and mocked me. Undaunted, when the men returned that evening, I repeated the story only to be met with the same ridicule. There was no such animal, they all said. Maybe my great hunger was making me see the things I wished to see.

Holding back my tears, I sulked in the depth of the cave, I was so sure of what I had seen. It was much later that the old man came in, for he could not keep up with the younger ones any longer. Amidst much joking they told him the story of the five-legged monster, but the old man did not laugh. Instead he called me over and made me repeat my story. He seemed to recognise the description. Yes, he was sure this was an animal that he had once seen being hunted when he himself was young and lived in the far north. Probably it had been driven south by the harsh cold weather. What I had taken to be the fifth leg was actually its long nose that reached almost to the ground and what I thought were the horns were actually two huge curved teeth. Gigantic and dangerous, he assured us that its capture, although very difficult, would provide us with enough meat to last until the rest of the game returned with the warmer weather.

And so early on the following morning all the able-bodied men set out to hunt this great beast. Because I had spotted the animal I was allowed, for the very first time, to go on the hunt with them. I can still remember that great feeling of excitement and pride.

At the lakeside, after much searching, we found the giant lurking amongst the snow-covered trees. We all trembled with fear when we saw its great size. The old man told us that we would have to entice it into the marshy ground by the lake, where its heavy weight would trap the animal in the soft mud and slow it down, before it could be tackled successfully. I looked on in wonder as the men tried to coax the monster out from amongst the trees. The animal would not budge until two of the bravest of the men went right up to it and flung their wooden stakes at its swaying snake-like nose. Suddenly, with a tremendous roar the giant lifted its long nose into the air and with huge flapping ears rushed out at them. As it came it swept the ground with those two long white tusks and it was with one of these that it managed to hook one of the men and toss him far up into the air. The other man made straight for the marsh and the monster followed, but as soon as it reached the soft ground, its ponderous feet sank into the mud and it was unable to lift them out. Its ferocious struggles only caused it to sink deeper into the squelching morass and it was then that the rest of the men set upon it with their stakes and stones and after a great struggle managed to slay the monster. As I looked on at this great mass of steaming flesh that everyone was soon busy cutting up, I could not help feeling a great surge of pride. I had been proved right after all.

This was a long time ago and they, his people, were all dead now, for it was shortly afterwards that they first encountered the pallid, two-legged, almost hairless creatures. They had heard vague stories of these animals from those of their own kind who had been driven from their hunting grounds by them and the increasingly cold winters and had come to seek shelter on the great Rock. Tall, long-limbed and very fast, with an uncanny resemblance to themselves, even to the extent of using the skins of other animals to cover their bodies, they were ruthless killers. Not only had they taken all their game and driven them from their hunting grounds, but they had also set out to kill them. Every summer they would come to the Rock and systematically hunt them. His people had no chance, there were so many of these vile creatures. Up to now he had managed to evade them, as this great white mountain was his home and he knew every nook and cranny. Over the years though he had seen his family and all of the others living in the caves on the Rock killed. Now he was all alone.

Below the screaming creatures were getting nearer. He knew what he must do; it was better than to have all those pointed long sticks plunged into him. He waited until they were practically upon him and then he jumped. In an instant the wind was rushing at him, by him, through him, he could hardly breathe, the forest below was hurtling towards him and as he tossed around he saw it, the cave, and remembered again. The old man, the tusked monster, his long-lost sister Oona.

Oona was my sister and friend. Together we had scaled the big mountain on which we lived and explored its many caves and beaches. There was a big storm, the wind came roaring in from the sea where the sun rises and mountainous white-crested waves crashed remorselessly on the far shore. We were happy, for we knew that once the wind died down and the sea grew calmer, all the women and children would trek across the sandy dunes and down to the shore to scavenge the tide lines for whatever the storm had washed up.

We always prided ourselves on making the best finds. That last time we went far up the coast, much further than we had ever dared go. Here a great river pours its waters out into the sea, its brown muddy waters colouring the blue sea all around. As we were about to turn back empty-handed we saw it, a fat bloated boar, lying there on the beach just waiting for us, the first scavengers, to claim it.

We were wondering how we could take it back with us when we heard screaming sounds and, looking up, saw a group of strange animals rushing towards us. Tall, two-legged, pale-skinned and very thin, they looked repulsive. It was the first time we had seen these creatures and they were to hound our lives henceforth. As the pack rushed towards us, we took to our heels. I made for the dense forest, but Oona, obedient to our elders' instructions, ran down to the sea. When attacked by an animal near the shore and the sea is calm, get into it and walk as far out as you can. Many a life had been saved in this way, as most animals fear the water.

The creatures, ignoring me, turned towards her, but long-legged Oona quickly made it into the water. Looking out from between the trees, I realised apprehensively that if they wished they could easily go in for her, as they were much taller. At the shoreline they appeared to hesitate and I breathed a sigh of relief; maybe they were as afraid of the water as the big cats were. However after a while two of the larger creatures plunged into the sea. Poor Oona was soon caught and the creatures on the shore jumped and cried as if with joy. She was speedily rushed out for far across the water black fins swiftly cut the surface – the sharp-toothed fish were coming. Still shouting and leaping in triumph, the pack left, bearing with them a kicking and struggling Oona and the bloated boar.

This was my first meeting with these cruel animals. Slowly I trudged homewards weighed down now by the prospect of having to tell the elders of the loss of my sister.

Poor Oona, who knows what dreadful fate awaited her.

At the foot of the cliff the last of the cavemen lay dead. He would never see the group of angry young men on that steep ridge. Had he been able to, he might have imagined he discerned in a couple of the swarthier ones a fleeting resemblance to his long-lost sister Oona. Soon scavengers would pick the shattered bones clean. Only the skull remained intact, to be covered eventually by debris from the rock face towering above. Many thousands of years were to go by before it would resurface again. Even then it would lie in some forgotten cabinet of a dusty museum for another sixteen years before this strange skull with its receding forehead and prominent eyebrows would be recognised for what it was.

The Ibex Hunt

3

3,000 BC

This was my special place. In the winter, the mighty river gushes its brown waters into the turbulent sea, but when the rains cease, the rolling sand dunes at its mouth stop the waters and form a wide lagoon. Then, in the hot dry summers, as the waters recede, the shrinking pools along the banks teem with fish. It was here that I came to hunt. I was not alone in harvesting this rich bonanza, for blue herons would stand tall and immobile in the shallow waters, waiting and watching before snapping at the passing multitude of fish. Sometimes, with a swooping dive, the fish eagle would come hurtling out of the sky to grab a fat mullet in its powerful talons.

Now and again I ventured across the river. I knew every sandbank and shoal and in late summer managed the crossing, even when the water reached up to my neck. It was risky, for here lived tribes that were enemies of my people, but I was not afraid.

The banks on that side were steeper with only occasional breaks forming deep pools and it was at one of these that I saw her for the first time. She was all alone and washing in one of the pools. Her long jet-black hair gleamed in the sunlight as she leaned over the still waters. She looked up and, seeing me, was gone in a flash, but in that instant, when we looked into each other's eyes, I had seen how beautiful she was.

I crossed the river every day after that and was about to despair of ever seeing her again when I spotted her, only this time she did not run but stood and stared back. It was thus that we became friends first and lovers soon after. I was infatuated with her and lived only for those precious moments across that broad river. Using the few words that we had in common we built up a language of our own and it was with this that I learnt that she was promised to the elder of one of the villages further up the coast. We were desperate and there and then decided to run away together, but where to?

I told her then of my other favourite hiding place, the Rock of the Ibexes, and took her down to the mouth of the river and showed her, in the distance, the sharp ridged mount that rose from the sea. The next day we were gone, trekking south along interminable sandy beaches until we reached the end of the land. There, just a short distance out from the shore lay the great Rock, rising almost vertically from the sea. I led her carefully across the shallow stretch of water that separated the rocky island from the mainland. I had already decided where we would hide, a small cave on a secluded rock ledge high above the beaches. And so we lived on here, ensconced in our passion for each other. We fed on the shellfish that we gathered together on the rocks by the shore, on the fish that I caught in the sea and on the plants that she collected on the steep slopes.

Soon she was with child and I worried as I saw her grow big. How would we manage all alone up here? She just smiled and assured me that even animals had their young on their own without any help. The night the pain started I watched fearfully as her struggles increased and her anguished cries grew louder. She pushed and writhed and suffered throughout that long night whilst I looked on frightened and helpless until finally, in the early morning, the baby was born. It was lifeless and my desperate efforts at reviving it were futile. All that day she held it to her breast and cried until, in the late evening, the blood came, and she herself died. I buried her just there, deep where no animal could ravage her, still clutching the child in her arms. Their bodies I covered with those small sweet-smelling white flowers which cover the Rock at this time of the year and of which she was so fond. Throughout that winter, with my sorrow and memories, I stayed on in the cave. Sometimes I imagined I could hear her calling me from the beach or I would see her running down the slope with her glistening black hair blowing in the wind. Eventually, exhausted and lonely, I returned to my village.

It was always just after the longest day in the year that the men from all the villages along the coast would gather at the foot of the giant Rock for the annual ibex hunt. The goats had given birth to their kids by then and not only would these hamper their movements, but the tender young would make excellent eating. Even the tribesmen from beyond the great river came. Normally sworn enemies, there seemed to be an undeclared truce for the hunt. It was essential to have large numbers of men for the drive to work properly and most years there were so many of these wild goats killed that there were more than enough for all.

The hunt would begin on the red sand slopes where the grass was always lush and the ibex gathered to feed on it. A long line of men was then formed to beat the undergrowth and drive the animals towards the precipices near the end of this big Rock. Sometimes they were lucky and would capture the odd boar that had strayed onto the island from the mainland at low tide or even the occasional deer, but their main quarry was the ibex which were so plentiful on the Rock. This annual slaughter did not seem to have much effect on the herds as so many always managed to get away.

Sometimes one of the men would be badly injured on the steep rocks and it was not unknown for a hunter to fall to his death, but the catch was always impressive and worth the effort. The goats would provide them not only with meat, but also hides for their clothes and horns for tools and decorations.

The old man was more of a hindrance than a help now, but he still insisted on coming to the hunt every year. After the hunt the boys would follow him furtively as he scrambled with difficulty up the steep slopes until he came to the ledge. At the small cave there, he would stand and staring out to sea would cry out a name that none of them could ever catch. It was always the same name and there was never any answer.

Phoenician Pioneers

4

1100 BC

Driven on by strong and persistent winds from the Levant, the slim, sharp-beaked vessel sped along the rugged coast. The long deep swells lifted the ship and rushed it helplessly forward only to wallow momentarily in vacuous troughs. To the south, purple mountains came rolling out of Africa towards them before plunging sharply into the turbulent sea. Northwards, as the dark night gave way to early dawn, they could just make out another distant shoreline and then, as the sun rose behind them and the coasts abruptly converged, they saw them. Gleaming white in the morning sunlight the two towering mounts of Melqart guarding the gates to where the waters meet the firmament. Those who passed through would never return. So it was said and the men quaked in fear, but their captain, noted for his great courage, was undaunted and determined to find out once and for all. There were rumours of lands beyond full of gold, silver and other metals. If this was so, great riches awaited those who dared.

Disregarding the mutterings of discontent amongst the crew, the captain tenaciously ploughed on, bravely crossing over to the alien northern shore. As they broke through the Strait, the land on either side opened out into an immense ocean and, hugging the coast and battling with the strong easterly winds, they sailed northwards past long beaches backed by huge mounds of sand. The land seemed to go on and on with no safe place for them to shelter during the coming night. They were about to turn back in desperation when they came upon a long narrow island guarding a large inlet, an ideal anchorage, as they were soon to realise and be grateful for.

On the following day, a terrible storm came roaring at them from the very edge of the world, where the red sun sets. Huge waves, the like of which they had never seen before, crashed mightily against the sandy shore, sending plumes of swirling spray deep into the calm waters of the lagoon. Sheltering here they were safe, but there were many of the crew, cowering on their rough wooden benches, who thought they had ventured into the abode of the damned and would never get back home.

Landing parties were sent ashore to search for fresh water and food. When they returned they reported that they had met the local tribesmen. These natives had shown them where they could obtain the best water and had even offered them food. Some of the men had noticed that those who seemed to be chiefs were copiously decorated with what appeared to be silver trinkets. This had caused great excitement. The following morning the captain himself went ashore to see for himself and met up with these chiefs. He soon ascertained that it was silver and what is more, he was able to learn that this metal was mined in the surrounding hills. The natives were friendly and appeared amenable to trade. They talked of large settlements further up the coast. It was now imperative that they get back to report on this great treasure. Their present anchorage was the perfect place to set up a trading depot. The storm could not last forever.

It lasted for ten days and they had to wait a further three for the great swells, which crashed onto the beaches, to subside. As soon as they considered it safe they set sail for home. Alas, no sooner had they entered the mouth of the narrows than the westerly wind came raging at them again with a vengeance, the roaring wind tearing at their sail and ripping it to pieces. The ship was carried forward helplessly past a wild inhospitable shoreline that sent out long fingers of sharp rocks which threatened at any moment to tear it apart. It was with great relief that they saw a wide bay opening up before them. Across it, through the flying spray, they could just see the giant Rock guarding the gates on the northern shore like a huge recumbent lion and beyond that, their very own longed-for sea.

However, the wind was not about to let them shelter in this bay and despite the strenuous efforts of the rowers, they were soon scurrying across towards the waiting jagged rocks at the base of that lion mountain. There was no let-up and they realised that nothing could save them; their ship would soon be smashed to pieces as the huge waves broke at the foot of the cliffs. Was this to be the angry gods' retribution for their rash action in breaching the forbidden gates? Then, as if by magic, they were gripped by a strong current, whipped round the end of the jutting Rock and suddenly found themselves in a small oasis of calm water in the lee of the mountain. Ahead they saw a tiny strip of sand onto which the oarsmen, straining with their last remaining strength, just managed to beach their battered vessel and then haul it up the shelving shore to safety.

It had been a miraculous escape and the sailors, prostrated on the beach, cried and prayed to the gods in gratitude for their salvation. It was quite a while before, recovering from their exhaustion, they could examine their landing place. Steep-sided and apparently unclimbable rocks hemmed them in on this narrow spit. Then, as the heavens seemed to break and torrents of rain fell upon them, they spotted a great cavern at the head of the beach. They all made for this and were soon ensconced in this cave, thankful for the shelter it provided from the inclement weather.

The cave was large, like a great temple, and indeed in a way it was destined to become a sort of shrine for them. Two days later, when the sea had finally calmed down and before they sailed away homewards, they placed the image of their goddess there and proffered votive offerings of thanksgiving for their miraculous salvation. In the years to come, their countrymen set up trading posts along the coasts of the great ocean beyond the Strait, not only at Gadir, in their sheltered lagoon anchorage which soon became famous, but all the way up to the Tin Islands, in the far north, where the yellow-haired tribes live. Even then many a passing ship would anchor in this tiny cove at the tip of the majestic white Rock to make offerings in gratitude for a safe passage to the statue of their goddess Astarte, left behind in the cavern by those first brave pioneers.

Carthago

5

300 BC

The early morning mist lay thick on the sea covering the coastal waters. In the distance, muffled sounds of throbbing booms followed quickly by the splash of dipping oars in perfect unison could be heard approaching fast. Suddenly the great ship burst out of the enveloping cloud, a mighty Carthaginian quadrireme, gathering momentum as it sped over the windless sea. The low pulsating beat of the large drum paced the rhythm of the rowers, interrupted now and again by the sharp staccato slap of the whiplash on the brown backs of the straining slaves. Straight for the narrows they steered. Ahead the dawn sun lit up the steep Rock face, making it shine white and sparkling. To them it was the prominent headland guarding the gates which only they were allowed to enter. Beyond the jagged Rock, through the hazy mist, they could just make out that other domed mount on the far shore, the other guardian of these gates. Once past the Rock promontory, they knew that they would be ensconced within its wide bay, sheltered from winds and currents.

Sure enough, as they swung round the base of the steep rocky cliffs that rose sharply from the sea at the tip of the headland, slicing seemingly effortlessly through the swirling eddies, they beheld the smooth grey waters of the bay, shadowed from the sun by the looming Rock. In the distance, at the head of the bay and beyond the Rock's shadow, the cluster of houses around their rich trading post could be seen glittering in the sunlight. The great vessel skimmed over the flat sea as the rhythm of the drumbeats increased, forcing the exhausted rowers, urged on by yet more lashes, into a final spurt.

Just as the ship gathered speed, a long sleek vessel was spotted, sneaking out of one of the small coves where it had been trying to hide in the sunless waters at the base of the overhanging cliffs. It was quickly identified as yet another of the Roman ships from the Etruscan region. Of late a few of these audacious trespassers had been found in this Strait. For one moment the intruding vessel seemed to be going to slip out and past the great ship, but the Carthaginians were adept seamen and masters of these seas. In a flash, with shouted orders and furious drumbeats, the mighty vessel seemed to turn on itself and then spurt towards the fleeing craft. Seeing the larger vessel almost towering above them, the small ship seemed to falter and in that fatal moment the sharp bronze beak of the Carthaginian vessel crashed into its wooden side, almost severing the smaller vessel in two.

It was over quickly. Amidst the cries of its rowers still chained to their benches, the Roman vessel sank, taking them with it. All that remained on the surface were the smashed timbers with some of the sailors clinging desperately on. It was just a question now of picking up these men, for they would serve well as rowers in the galleys. No one must be allowed to carry news of these rich lands and seas back to their homeland. This was the private domain of Carthage: the secret narrows where the giant tuna swam and the lands beyond, rich in silver, tin and much else. They allowed no ships beyond this Strait.

Soon the great Carthaginian vessel turned again and, as if nothing untoward had occurred, headed straight for Karteia, its captains confident that they had helped preserve their empire. Within a hundred years though, and after three long and bitter wars, these lands and seas were to be wrested from them by that very same upstart ambitious state of Rome. Even their own capital, Carthage, the home port of this great vessel, would eventually be razed to the ground by the victorious Romans.

Defeat at Munda

6

45 BC

Desperately the brothers rode, fleeing from the carnage as they escaped the site of their devastating defeats. South toward the Strait they galloped, through the thickly forested country. It was as they left the mountains and neared the small town of Lauro Vetus (Alhaurin de la Torre) that Gnaeus, wounded in the battles and lagging behind, was overtaken by his pursuers and killed. Late in the afternoon, as Sextus and his small band of loyal soldiers breached the last hill, they beheld the mighty Rock of Calpe rising sharply from the sea and the serrated range of mountains of Mauretania beckoning from across the narrow Strait. Hidden amongst the trees, they stopped to decide on their best route. At the head of the bay lay Carteia. It was near here that Caesar had landed after crossing the Strait with his legions, and availing himself of the natural hot springs in the hills nearby, had rested them for the coming campaign in the mountains beyond. This town, a Colonia Libertinorum, settled by veteran legionaries, had closed its gates against Caesar. Sextus knew that many here had fought in his father's campaigns and had always been loyal to the Pompeys. News of the defeat at Munda must be spreading fast though, and he was well aware that there is nothing like a battle lost to change people's allegiances. So they were wary as they entered the town. Realising that the town officials were decidedly nervous, and suspecting that there were divisions amongst them, Sextus made plans to leave before they were betrayed.

A few days later, with the Carteians still debating what should be done with them, they left stealthily at night, crossed to the far side of the narrow isthmus and, with the heavy seas pounding the beach behind them, finally reached the vertical face of the Rock. They skirted behind this, climbing up the steep sand slopes. Then down into the small sheltered bay where, in the shallow caves at the back of the beach, the few fishermen who harvested this rich sea lived. His father had landed here once during the campaign to rid the Mediterranean of pirates and had told his sons of these far-off hideaways. Sextus was sure that he could persuade some of these hardy and independent men to take them across the Strait and out of Hispania. It was their only chance. On the other side he knew that his family still had many followers and they would have a better chance of getting away, maybe even to raise another army.

The fishermen readily agreed – for a price. They gave allegiance to no man, but would not leave until the Levant wind, which was blowing strongly at the time, changed. For two days they waited nervously. At night Sextus reflected on the long campaign and the final battle which had sealed their fate. It had been a close thing and the outcome was in the balance until the very end, but then, in the confusion of the struggle, orders had been misinterpreted and the wily Caesar had seen his chance. Their brave legions had been decimated in one of the bloodiest battles they had ever fought. Despite this terrible setback, he was determined to continue the struggle to defeat the brutal and ambitious Caesar and avenge his father's death in Egypt.

On the third day, the wind appeared to be changing, but still the fisherman would not set off. By way of explanation they led the soldiers up the steep cliffs at the southern end of the peninsula and showed them why. There in the lee of the Rock, waiting for the wind to change to set sail for Rome, were seven Roman vessels, anchored and protected from the mountainous swells which could, and often did, wrench them from their anchors.

The following day the westerly wind finally blew and, hiding in the fishermen's shelters, they counted as the heavy transports sailed past on their way home. That night they were ferried across the Strait to Mauretania, close behind they could just make out the lights of some vessels in hot pursuit. They managed to beach their boat on a deserted cove and Sextus, eluding his pursuers, escaped to fight another day. He was to outlive Caesar's assassination on the Ides of March of the following year, almost a year to the day of the battle at Munda.

After a varied career of alliances, piracy and deceit, Sextus, the last of the sons of Pompey the Great, was finally cornered and killed at Miletus in Asia Minor by the Roman General Marcus Titius in 35 BC.

The Hermit

7

178 AD

The sharp pungent smells of the garum pits to the west of the town permeated the quayside that hot summer evening as the heavily laden Roman cog docked. It was in the eighteenth year of the reign of the Emperor Marcus Aurelius, nearly a hundred and eighty years after the birth of Christ, that John of Antioch arrived at Carteia. He had fled the persecutions of the followers of the Cristos in his hometown. Endeavouring to put as much distance between himself and Rome from whence the edicts for the persecution of this new and rapidly spreading religion were emanating, he had boarded the first available vessel at the coast.

He knew no one here and eventually found lodgings in one of the many sailors' inns along the seafront. He searched high and low but could find no one of the faith, so for the next month he endeavoured, without much success, to teach his new religion to the bawdy crowds who lived along this waterfront. This was a boisterous and thriving town, famous throughout the Empire for its tuna products. It was said that the garum from Carteia, that piquant fish sauce made from the fermented entrails of the giant tuna of the Strait, was the best in the Empire. Especially that produced from the spring run when the fish, returning after fattening in the great ocean, entered the Mediterranean in prime condition.

He despaired of gaining any converts here and determined to sail on out into the great ocean and take the message to the Roman lands further north, maybe even to the barbarians themselves. However, before doing so he decided to visit the countryside around the town and it was as he was passing out through the gates that he saw it. There was no mistaking it; there amidst the inevitable graffiti on the lower parts of the city walls was the sketch of a fish. The Ichthus, the fish symbol, sign of the

Galilaeans. He realised then that it was here amongst the very poor and simple people that he should have looked, for was it not amongst these that Christ had first preached? He searched for a long time before he found them. They were just a small group who had fled from Rome itself two years earlier and settled here outside the town walls amidst the tall mounds of crushed Murex seashells, the bleached discarded remnants of the lucrative purple dye trade. With this small congregation he commenced his ministry and soon the message spread amongst the poor.

By the time the edicts requiring the Christians to make offerings to the Roman gods really started to be enforced at Carteia, he had a large following. Many of these poor people who refused to thus apostate their faith were soon rounded up in the ensuing persecutions, imprisoned and even put to death for their beliefs. Those who remained urged John to flee the city before he too was caught. Reluctant to leave his flock, he was finally forced to go when the soldiers started demolishing the hutments in an effort to root him out. One dark night, fearful and penniless, he set out into the unknown. He knew that the soldiers would pursue him relentlessly and as he awoke on that first morning of his flight, desperate and afraid, he looked across the bay and beheld the great grey rock of Calpe topped with an almost perfect halo of cloud. He took this as a sign from God and determined there and then to seek refuge within this rocky mount.

And so it was that John spent the rest of his life as a hermit in one of the caves near the top of this craggy peninsula. He survived many attempts at his capture and despite the constant cruel persecutions ministered to the ever-growing Christian converts around the bay. In later years they would make pilgrimages to this small cave even long after his death.

He was nearly eighty years old when, rising early one bright morning, he beheld a fearsome sight. Far up the Levant coast, where the curving yellow beaches meet the broad Barbesula (Guadiaro) river, he could just make out the ships and on the shore, at the small settlement, the fishermen's houses were going up in flames. He had heard of the rogue pirate fleets that were devastating the towns along the coast. He must warn Carteia and so, despite the danger to himself, he immediately set off down and across the isthmus.

He scrambled down the steep slope, the thorns tearing at his thinly fleshed limbs, and as he struggled along the sandy beach, his strength began to ebb and he begged his God to allow him just enough time to reach the town gates and warn its people, the very people who had persecuted his flock for so long. Finally, exhausted and practically crawling the last few yards, he reached the gates and delivered his warning to the guards there. As soon as these soldiers realised who he was, he was clapped in irons and the governor informed. The orders came immediately: he was to be imprisoned while the governor decided on a suitable form of execution that would serve as a warning to his followers and put an end to this contemptible superstition.

That night, as the old man lay on the cold stone floor of the small rat-infested cell into which he had unceremoniously been thrown, he asked his God, 'Why?'. Why had He made him come to warn these enemies of his people? For he now realised that such a town had nothing to fear from a few pirate ships. He even began to suspect that there had been no ships at all and it had all been a figment of the befuddled mind of an old man. Why? What was the purpose of it all?

Early in the morning, the captain of the guard came to inform the governor that word of the imprisonment of the Hermit of the Mount was spreading and crowds were beginning to form outside the city walls. The governor immediately ordered that the old man be put to the sword to quell any further disturbance. When the guards entered the cell they found that they were too late. The hermit's God had already called him home. His frail body lay on that filthy stone floor, just mere skin and bones, but with a sublime look on his gnarled, brown face just as if, before setting off on his final journey, he had been given the answer he sought.

Later that morning, as the governor patrolled the walls he was perturbed to see the crowds of people coming from far and near and gathering into a menacing mob. He promptly ordered the gates to be closed. He was much surprised on his return to the palace to see that crowds were also beginning to form within the town, in the central square. These Christians seemed to be everywhere. Maybe he had misjudged the extent of their following. What really tipped the scales for this noble Roman though was when, as he was about to call out the legion to quell this motley uprising, his own wife and daughters came crying to him, urging him to desist. He realised then. From that day the persecution of the Christians in this corner of the vast empire ceased.

Decline of Empire

8

363 AD

I was the quartermaster general for the imperial town of Carteia when I was ordered north to Gades, Malaca and even Corduba to try to seek funds to pay the legion stationed in our town. This had become a recurrent problem in the last few years and had given rise to much discontent. This time though the situation was much more serious, there was no money anywhere in Baetica and communications with the rest of the Empire were becoming increasingly difficult.

We were returning home tired and empty-handed and it was with sinking hearts that we saw the columns of grey smoke rising into the sky as we neared the town. What I most dreaded had happened. The legionaries, now mostly uncouth barbarian recruits from the north, had revolted. I feared for my wife and children. I soon learnt that they had perished in the uprising. Bands of wild men were now looting the town and ravaging the surrounding areas and it was with extreme difficulty that we managed to evade them.

Where could we hide from these savages? Then I remembered the Herculean cave at Calpe. An ideal hiding place, where we could shelter indefinitely and indeed even defend ourselves in those tortuous caverns should we be found. There were seven of us. Fortunately, one of my subalterns had lived at the base of this great Rock as a boy and knew the cave well. It was indeed a wonder to behold. Narrow passages opened out into great halls. From the ceiling descended columns of coloured rock, some to be met by similar ones rising from the ground, the whole resembling a magical forest of stone. There was even talk of a beautiful underground lake deep inside. The cave was halfway up the mount and from this vantage-point we could see the burnt-out ruins of our town. Although marauding groups of rebels would sometimes come to the

Rock, there was little chance of them finding us in this excellent hiding place.

It was ten days later that the rebels, no doubt having run out of food, finally left for the north. I pitied anyone who lay in their path. Cautiously we descended onto the beach and approached the town. From here and there, other survivors appeared. The town itself was deserted. As the only remaining senior officer, I took command as decreed in Imperial Orders.

Over the next few months and with the help of the surviving citizens, we managed to restore some semblance of order, repairing many of the buildings that had not been too badly damaged in the revolt. We tried to seek help from the towns to the north but there was confusion everywhere and no help came. I also sent messages to the emperor in Milano, both by land and by sea, with a record of what had happened and the steps I was taking to rehabilitate the city. I even began to take pride in the work I was doing and dared to hope that in recognition of this I might be offered some substantial promotion. This might help me rebuild my shattered life.

Time passed, but no reply came. Eventually, six months after the revolt, the lookouts on top of Calpe spied ships approaching from the east and sent messages to the town that there were ten war galleys on their way. It seemed rather a large fleet, but it could be that they were sending loyal reinforcements. However, I feared the worst for these were chaotic times in the Empire. By mid-afternoon these fears increased as we learnt that the ships, instead of rounding the white Rock and coming into port here, were landing their troops at the sandy beaches on the far side of the isthmus. I immediately sent emmisaries to greet them, but again we waited in vain. There was no reply. They did not return.

That evening, as the light from the setting sun speckled the blue-grey waters of the bay, my worst fears were confirmed. A Roman legion in full battle order with gleaming imperial eagles held aloft marched in and promptly took control of the town. Completely ignored until the very last moment, I was then handed an Imperial order by the newly-appointed provincial governor in command. Charged with open rebellion against the emperor, I was to be summarily executed or I could opt for a more honourable death by my own hand. There was to be no appeal.

In the gathering dusk, Lucius Sempronius Palas, embittered by the world's seemingly random ingratitude and injustice, drew his sword and ended his own life. Perhaps it was best that before he died he did not realise that amongst the centurions at the head of the newly-arrived legion, now on parade in the square below, stood some of the leaders of the revolt of his own legion.

The Vandals

9

411 AD

It was just over two years ago now that their nightmare had started; for it was then that they had first heard of the Vandals. This savage tribe from lands far beyond the old Empire had broken through the mountain passes in the north and were devastating the country. In vain they had hoped and prayed that this would be yet another seasonal incursion and the marauding tribes would return to their lands once they were sated. After all, this was happening very far away. But inexorably the hordes kept on coming. For the past year, the refugees from the north had been arriving, bringing harrowing tales of the atrocities committed by the barbarians, of whole towns looted and burnt to the ground, the inhabitants put to the sword. Every day more of these bedraggled people arrived. Some brought meagre possessions, but most were empty-handed and all were terrified. Now the village, set in the old Roman town of Carteia, was overflowing and the new arrivals were tearing down more and more of the remaining derelict buildings to put up makeshift homes for themselves. Down by the beach, the once renowned Roman harbour was all but obliterated by the encroaching sea and sands.

Each morning their little church was packed with scared supplicants praying for salvation from this scourge of the devil that was fast descending upon them. At night families would huddle together, mothers crying and holding onto their children, fearful of what might befall them, the men trying to calm them with what they knew were false hopes. Nor was there the remotest chance of any help coming from distant Rome. The Empire was in tatters and only the elderly in the village remembered the marching legions. The news now was that, having destroyed the towns immediately to the north, the barbarians would be upon them within a week or two. Lookouts had been posted atop the nearby hills. Each morning the frightened elders would congregate in the open square at the centre of the village and argue incessantly about what was to be done. All agreed that resistance would be futile, some proposed that they should throw themselves upon the mercy of the invaders, but the refugees told them that the barbarians had no mercy. They had seen this tried in many towns before, only to be followed by a general massacre. Now there was nowhere else left to run to. Some suggested sailing across the water to the mountainous country across the Strait, but those who owned the few available boats had already fled with their families. Little did they know that the Vandals would follow them there one day.

In the end, when horsemen rode in saying that the arrival of the hordes was imminent, people started fleeing into the countryside, to the forests, canyons, wherever they could hope to evade their pursuers. Many though, looked across at the great White Mountain, the Mons Calpe, and hoped that it would provide them with refuge. It was the furthest south that they could go. There were stories of huge caverns there where they could hide.

That night, taking as much food as they could carry, the remaining villagers fled along the beach towards the great Rock. In the morning, as they climbed the lower slopes of the mountain and looked back, they could see the smoke rising from what had been their village. They had to find the caves without delay. It was with growing fear though that, towards the afternoon, as they frantically searched, they saw the mounted barbarians leave the smouldering ruins of the village and head towards the Rock. Now it became imperative that the caverns be found, but there was no one amongst them who knew their whereabouts. In horror they clambered and fled southwards. In between the crying of the children and the shrieks of the women, the yells of the pursuing horsemen could be heard. On they went until they reached the top of the headland at the very end of the Rock. Below, the frothing sea broke against the foot of the high cliffs. There they huddled until the barbarians burst out on to the flat land at the tip of the peninsula and with mighty yells rushed towards them. Now their priests and friars stepped forward and, holding the Christian crosses aloft, beseeched their pursuers to show pity on their flock. In horror the frightened villagers saw them mercilessly set upon and it was then that these desperate and terrified people turned and started jumping off the cliff. Soon men and women, many clutching their children, were plunging down to certain death. It was all over quickly and when the horsemen reached the top of the precipice there was hardly anyone left there. Furious and impotent, the barbarians stood on the edge of the cliffs and looked down at the floating bodies as they were smashed on to the rocks at the base by the raging seas.

It is ironic that of all the settlers, invaders, conquerors and colonists that have passed through here, it was to be these uncouth and barbaric Vandals, whose very name has become a synonym for wanton destruction, who bequeathed their name to this beautiful land – Vandalus – Andalucia. Only after they had exhausted the resources of this rich land were they finally ousted from here by the Goths and crossed the Strait into Africa.

Gibel Tarik

10

711 AD

At the end of April, the great Rock lay somnolent in the early morning half-light surrounded by its circle of sea. As the balmy sou'westerly wind climbed the slope and the moisture collected during its long journey across the Atlantic condensed, the white wispy cloud formed seemed to cover the top half of the Rock in a woolly cloak. It was almost deserted now. Even the few fishermen that came in spring and summer to its small coves and beaches to fish its rich waters had left, driven off by the constant raids from across the Strait. As dawn broke, a small flotilla of heavily-laden ships set out from the opposite coast heading towards it. Who could foretell then that their coming would change the course of history and in the process baptise this Rock with a new name, a name it would retain for posterity?

All that night the hard work of getting the troops and particularly the horses onto the ships had gone on. The troops were apprehensive, hardened warriors though they were. They had no experience of the sea and were uneasy at being tightly packed in these frail-looking ships floating on these unfamiliar waters.

As the skies lightened, the heavily-laden ships set off on their short but perilous crossing. Ahead they could just make out the dark shadow that was the distant coastline. On board, the jostling and neighing of the horses, nervous and unaccustomed to the swaying movements and fearful at being cooped up, added to the anxiety of the troops. Their captain had insisted that the horses and their riders be divided amongst all the ships, so that if any ship was lost he would not be totally deprived of his precious cavalry, his strongest weapon.

This captain was the Berber commander, Tarik ibn-Ziyad, a freedman of the emir of the Moorish armies in Africa, Musa ibn-Nosayr, and entrusted by him with the task of leading this raid on al-Andalus.

The morning was well advanced when the small fleet entered the broad bay. An ebbing tide had nudged them towards the western shore and along the coast they could already make out the horsemen racing to give the alarm. As the ships approached the first beach they came to and started to prepare for landing, they saw the Visigoth cavalry galloping out from the old Roman port of Albus (Algeciras).

Tarik realised that he had no chance of putting his troops ashore safely. To try to land now with the enemy on the beach could be disastrous. He needed an almost deserted beach to make a successful landing and the element of surprise was essential to enable him to disembark some of his troops, especially the horses. Once these were ashore, he was sure the cavalry could establish a secure beachhead.

He sailed out again into the middle of the bay. To the north, at the head of the bay he espied another suitable beach stretching between two broad rivers. Surmising that it would take the enemy some time to cross either of these, he made for this beach. They had hardly started preparations for landing when the enemy cavalry again turned up on the sands. Unknown to the Moors, the river was spanned by a wooden bridge further upstream. Reluctantly the invading fleet sailed out again into the bay. It was late afternoon by now and after loitering there for some time, they set sail southward.

The Visigoth governor Theodomir and his captains congratulated themselves on having repelled yet another raid, this time a really large one. Belatedly they sent a detachment of troops to the Rock across the bay to establish a lookout there and keep an eye on the retreating enemy fleet. It was a long and gruelling climb to the top of the Rock and by the time the small force had reached the summit, darkness had set in.

The following morning, as soon as there was enough light, they started searching the seas for the alien ships, but there was no sign of them. They checked the rugged coastline directly below them at the base of the precipice and were relieved that there was no sign of the raiders there either. Then one of them pointed northwards. Down there in the corner, just visible from their lofty lookout and tucked into the base of the Rock, the enemy ships were busy landing their troops and horses on to the marshy ground of the isthmus that separated the Rock from the mainland. With heavy hearts the soldiers lit their beacons for they feared that it would be too late.

Tarik was full of confidence now that he had his men and especially his cavalry on land. It was wonderful to feel the solid earth beneath his feet. Quickly he sent out parties to reconnoitre the surrounding areas and particularly the large Rock. They were to search for a suitable place to build a fort, for Tarik was determined to establish a permanent base from where he could keep in contact with his countrymen across the Strait and receive reinforcements if needed. An ideal site for such a stronghold, half way up the mount and facing the enemy port across the bay was soon identified. He promptly started his men on the task of building this fort. Meanwhile, attempts by the enemy to dislodge them from the Rock were easily fended off. However he soon realised that the building of this fortress was going to be arduous and the time taken would allow the enemy to send for reinforcements from the north.

Always a daring and incisive leader, Tarik decided to attack the towns of the hinterland and immediately set off to conquer these. Portus Albus, on the other side of the bay was stormed and quickly taken, as was the fort on the green island in front of it. Further along the coast lay Julia Traducta. His countryman Tarif abu-Zarah had successfully raided this port the previous year. It would eventually take his name, Tarifa. This also had a strongly fortified island, but it soon fell to Tarik's valiant warriors. These ports were to provide him with the solid base, which he was seeking. He then sent for reinforcements from across the Strait.

The new Gothic king, Roderick, was in the Basque country in the far north quelling another insurrection in his belligerent kingdom when he heard the news of the invasion. He had hardly had a moment's peace since his coronation and even that had been plagued with disorder. He was the duke of Baetica when Witiza, king of the Visigoths in Iberia, died, some say under suspicious circumstances. After many tribulations Roderick persuaded or coerced most of the nobles to proclaim him as the new king, bypassing the rightful heir to the throne, the late king's son, Aquila. Many in his kingdom still considered him a usurper and it is possible that the disgruntled sons of Witiza may have encouraged the Muslims to cross the Strait.

Roderick set out at once for the south, gathering as many troops as he could on the way. By the time he reached the southern coast, he had a vast army, though many of these would not prove to be totally loyal when it came to the battle. Some of the discontents, under the mistaken belief that this was just another raid and the Moorish invaders were only interested in booty and would return to their country eventually, actually changed sides during the battle. Unaware of this, the king was confident of victory as he deployed his troops on the low hills along the banks of the Guadalete river where it wound its sluggish way down to the Atlantic Ocean. The opposing army, with their flowing robes and white turbans, looked ragged and puny by comparison.

In the bloody and protracted battle that followed, Tarik, making clever use of his swift cavalry and the dissension amongst the enemy leaders, utterly destroyed the Visigoth army. Roderick's body was never found and no one really knows what became of him. Spain now lay at Tarik's feet: barely three months after the start of the invasion, the Moors were well on their way to the conquest of most of the Iberian peninsula.

The jealous Musa was to regret the appointment of his Berber ex-slave as commander when the dashing Tarik proved to be so successful. He had obviously intended, once a secure beachhead had been established and the strength of the enemy ascertained, to cross the Strait himself and lead the victorious armies to the conquest of the Western Peninsula. The following year, when the furious emir finally caught up with his conquering captain at Toledo, he is said to have struck him across the face with a whip in front of the troops. He promptly relieved him of his command and had him imprisoned. When the caliph in Damascus heard of this, he recalled both men. He stripped Musa, who he suspected of wanting to create his own power base in those far-off lands, of all his offices and imposed a heavy fine on him. Despite this, the memory of this great general and Commander of the Faithful who conquered most of North Africa for Islam lives on in the Strait in the name of the southern pillar of Hercules, Gibel Musa.

Behind him, on the great Rock where he had made his landing, Tarik had left a small party of workmen to finish off the fort he was building there. This was not the only thing he was to leave behind, for posterity was to bequeath his name to this Rock, the Mount of Tarik, Gibel Tarik – Gibraltar.

Madinat Al-Fath

11

1160 AD

The great Berber caliph of Morocco, Abd al-Mumin, decided to visit the kingdom which he had wrested from the Almoravids across the Strait. He sailed from Sebta and landed at the Gibel. He had already heard reports of this strategically-placed peninsula and had signified his intention to build a castle on it. Preliminary work on this had already commenced and he was eager to inspect its progress. As an astute general surveying the towering mass of the Rock surrounded almost completely by the sea, he was immediately impressed by its potential as a fortress. He was also acutely aware of its historical significance to his people. It was from this Rock bastion that his kinsman, the Berber Tarik ibn-Ziyad, had sallied forth with his army to capture the Western Peninsula for Islam and create the beautiful kingdom of al-Andalus. This had been achieved barely eighty years after the start of that amazing Arab conquest which swept out of Arabia into Asia Minor and across North Africa following the death of the Prophet. Now, having inspected the Rock's meagre defences and noted their sorry state of repair, he determined to carry through his original aim and make this stronghold impregnable and to build, within these defences, a city worthy of the Muslims' first landing in this country of the infidels.

At this time the Rock itself was called by some the Gibel al-Fath, the Mount of Victory and he determined to name his new city Madinat al-Fath, City of Victory. He then sent for the best engineers and architects in his kingdom. From Cordoba, Malaga, Granada and Seville they came. From this latter city came the famous architect Ahmad ibn-Basu who would later build the beautiful Patio de Naranjos there. Plans for the building of defensive walls, towers, mosques, baths and aqueducts were prepared. Even a windmill was to be built on top of the Rock to harness the power of the pernicious Levant wind. This splendid city was to be accessed via the great Bab al-Futuh, the Gate of Conquest, to be erected at the very foot of the Rock.

To ensure the proper execution of his plans, Al-Mumin decided to stay on the Rock for a time and supervise these works himself and he therefore sent to his homeland across the Strait for his wives. One of these was a young and beautiful girl, Aminah, herself a Berber and his favourite. She was the daughter of a chieftain from Barbary and he was infatuated with her. On some flat land on the southern slopes of the Rock, away from the city and bustle of the building works and surrounding a large well, he ordered a small palace to be built for her. He had gardens laid out around this and, to ensure that she would not pine for the stark beauty of her upland home on the Rif mountains, he had plants and trees brought from there. This garden he filled with the small fat partridges from her homeland of which he knew she was so fond. He even brought over a troop of the tailless monkeys that roamed the lands around her native village.

And so, under the watchful eye of this energetic Almohad caliph, the works continued. Unfortunately for the new city of Madinat al-Fath, within two months the native tribes along the southern fringe of his large kingdom rebelled and Al-Mumin had to leave for Africa to suppress the rebellion. He never returned and three years later he was dead. He left behind his son, Abu Said, the king of Granada, to supervise the works and ensure their completion. Said was not about to forgo the luxuries and splendour of the city of Granada for what was still just a frontier fortress, and the works were eventually abandoned. The Almohads were to hold sway in southern Spain until their disastrous defeat at Las Navas de Tolosa in 1212 AD at the hands of the Christians crippled their power.

Almost two centuries later, that famous Muslim traveller Ibn Battuta, returning from visiting his mother's grave in Tangier, came to the Rock. He records that there were few fortifications left from that era before the sultan of Fez Abu'l-Hassan built the great square castle keep we know today. At this time, the name Gibel al-Fath, the Mount of Victory, still lingered on. Today only the vestiges of walls remain to remind us of al-Mumin's unfinished works, but on the upper Rock the Barbary partridges and apes still roam as reminders of that bygone age. Most of the great mosque, with its own Patio de Naranjos, was built much later, but it has suffered considerable damage over the centuries. When the Spanish came it was consecrated as a Christian church and then further altered under the British. Nearly a thousand years were to go by before Gibraltar was embellished again with a truly beautiful mosque.

Sanctuary

12

1311 AD

Diego knew he was destined for the galleys, but he had had no alternative. His family was starving. That night in desperation he had gone into the royal hunting grounds and lain in wait by one of the many well-worn game tracks. Sure enough, during the darkest part of the night he heard them coming, a group of wild pigs grunting and rummaging in the undergrowth, nuzzling for the rich brown acorns that littered the leaf-strewn ground. He let them go by and then selected a fat sow that was lagging behind. With one leap he was on her and with a short sharp stab of his finely-honed knife he cut her throat. It was over quickly. He was not the village slaughterman for nothing. Unfortunately, hearing the noise, the boar rushed back and in one powerful lunge slashed his leg open. The ensuing commotion brought the gamekeepers to the spot and he was promptly taken into custody.

He languished in the jailhouse for a month. His leg healed, despite the squalid conditions. Now the rumours were that the prisoners would be taken to the port for placement in the galleys. He knew he would never survive this. Once as a young boy his father had taken him down to the waterfront at Cadiz and he had watched a galley come alongside. He saw the exhausted rowers slumped on their oars, stripped to the waist and chained to the benches, their bare backs still showing the bleeding welts where the whips had cut into them. The very memory had haunted him since his capture and he determined to make a run for it if the opportunity arose. It did that very night. A guard who was always drunk was on duty and, thinking that Diego was still unable to walk, had carelessly left the gate open. He was out and past the snoring man in a flash and was soon making for the mountains he knew so well.

Here he hid for some time and eventually was able to contact his family. He had heard of the amnesty given to prisoners who settled in the fort on the Rock of Gibraltar and realised that this was his only chance now. Two years earlier, this fortress had finally fallen to the Christian forces, bringing to an end almost six hundred years of Moorish occupation of the Rock. In an effort to repopulate his recent conquest, King Ferdinand IV of Castile had offered a free pardon to any criminal who resided in Gibraltar for one year and a day. He would try to obtain sanctuary there. Over the next fortnight, Diego slowly made his way through the forests towards the great Rock. Finally he came upon the wide bay with the tall mount looming up on the far side. That night he crossed the sandy isthmus and at first light, when the gates to the fort were opened, he attempted to enter. There were problems with the guards and over the next few days they tried to check his story. At first it seemed that he might be sent back, as the authorities at the fort were not sure whether the amnesty could be applied to anyone who wronged against the king. In the end he was allowed to stay.

He settled down on this bleak Rock and sent word to his family. He waited for months but they never came. Maybe they were afraid of coming to this coast where the constant raids by pirates or the Moors from across the Strait made life very perilous. It was this very danger that had prompted the king to encourage people to settle on the Rock with special inducements. Slowly Diego carved out a life for himself with a bit of fishing and gardening to augment his earnings as slaughterman.

It was during his fourth month here that he met her. Beaten and bruised by a drunken husband, in desperation Maria had taken advantage of King Ferdinand's edict, which also applied to women running from their husbands, and fled to the Rock. Soon they set up home together within the small town huddled below the castle and both decided to stay on even after their year and a day were up. Together they survived the siege three years later when, despite the fact that there were so few defenders, the town managed to hold out until the King sent reinforcements.

At this time the inhabitants of the Rock were few in numbers. They were a rough lot made up mainly of all manner of escaped convicts. Life was fraught with danger and the constant threat of raids from the sea made it all the more so. However, the very fact that there were so few people meant that the governor and his soldiers could keep a tight reign on them. Diego and Maria managed to live relatively peacefully and frugally within the confines of this small peninsula. At the slightest sign of danger they would quickly seek safety inside their walled town and if the threat materialised they would shelter within the castle itself.

Then, eighteen years later, the Moors came again, this time in much greater numbers and led by the very able one-eyed Abd'l Malik. Laying siege to the fortress, he quickly established his archers and siege engines along the top of the Rock and commenced a continuous and murderous barrage of stones and arrows down on the town. Soon Gibraltar was in a desperate situation. The corrupt governor, Vasco Perez de Meira, had squandered the money and even sold some of the arms intended for the town's defence. After a rigorous siege lasting only four months, during which the townspeople underwent extreme hardship, they were forced to capitulate and the Rock, after only twenty-four years, was recaptured by the Moors. Great was the consternation, considering that the Spanish king with a relieving army was only a few days' march away, when it was discovered that there were still substantial food supplies within the castle, including much of the grain brought in by the one ship that had managed to break through the blockade. The despicable governor had apparently been feeding this to his Moorish prisoners in the hope of obtaining better ransoms for them if he survived the siege or of ingratiating himself with the enemy if he was forced to surrender. As soon as the siege was over, he fled to Morocco.

Poor Diego's worst nightmare became a reality. Under the terms of surrender the inhabitants were allowed to leave, but he had been captured in the fighting before this. He never saw Maria again and ended up as a rower in a galley after all, only this time it was much worse for it was a Moorish galley.

Of Kings and Sieges

13

1344/1356 AD

Four years earlier at the Rio Salado, only half a league from Tarifa, the flower of our armies had been slaughtered. The river had flowed red with the blood of the thousands of our brave warriors who fell that day. In the sands of that accursed battlefield though was carved the fate of that persistent aggressor of our people, the Christian tyrant Adfunus, had he but known. Slowly but inexorably over the next few years his armies had kept on advancing until they were at the gates of our town and there they had stayed until we capitulated.

Will I ever be able to forget the pain and sorrow of that ill-fated day? After enduring twenty long months of siege, starvation, disease and death we had finally been forced to surrender our beloved al-Jazirah to these barbarous infidels and Adfunus, their brutal King Alfonso. He had been helped in this conquest by many chieftains from faraway northern countries. Even our brave soldiers' use of the new magic weapons that belch out fire and wreak destruction from afar had not saved us.

With my wives and children, taking only that which we could carry with us, we had trekked along the beaches that circle this bay to the last remaining bastion of Islam on this coast, the Gibel Tarik. From here we had watched helplessly as, across the bay, the flames destroyed our beloved town. On this great Rock our master the Sultan Abu'l-Hassan, after reconquering the citadel, had built numerous fortifications and walls and a great castle which would ensure that this fortress at least would never again be conquered by the idolaters. Maybe one day we would sally forth once again, like our brave Captain Tarik had done, and recapture our lost kingdoms in the Western Peninsula.

Barely five years after that tragedy he is back, this Alfonso, to besiege us yet again with his troops, trying to oust us from our new home on the Gibel. Many years earlier he tried to capture this fortress and failed, but he is a determined man. His ships have blocked the seas, allowing no succour to reach us from our compatriots across the Strait. We are alone and, although our mighty walls and castle protect us, we are slowly starving. On the narrow neck of land that lies at the foot of our Rock, his army grows ever larger and prepares to attack us once again. We can see the devilish machines he is constructing there to break our walls, and his own silken tents where he holds court.

Then, as if Allah had heard our piteous prayers, this evil monarch is struck down. That horror of horrors, the Black Death, has invaded his body and on the holiest day of his idol-worshipping religion, he dies. As the enemy army decamps and prepares to take the body of their dead king with them, our leaders, to show their mercy and compassion even to this relentless enemy of Islam, open the gates and emerge to stand in silence as the death cortege marches away. There is no fighting that day. Even as they go though, Pedro, the new king, is proclaimed there beneath our very walls. Maybe he will also come one day to try to oust us from our Rock, like his dead father.

Only six years of peace and tranquillity are allowed us. Now our own sultan, Abu Inan, he that rebelled against his own father the great Abu'l-Hassan and forced him to abdicate the throne, has appointed one of his brothers, the cruel Isa Ibn al-Hassan of ill repute, to be our governor. For three weeks the levanter blows unrelentingly, covering the mount with its canopy of low grey cloud and making the crossing of the Strait impossible. In these dank and humid conditions an air of foreboding permeates the town. At last, riding the long swells of the dying easterly wind, the first boat arrives and Ibn al-Hassan comes into our midst and our sorrows begin. Soon extortion, torture and death are rampant in our little town. Not content, this brutal governor unleashes his wild and sadistic son on us and life becomes intolerable. Desperate appeals to our sultan remain unanswered, for no doubt this ruler prefers to keep this evil and ambitious brother well away from his kingdom and across the Strait.

But worst is still to come. In Morocco the tribes rise up against the sultan and we vainly hope that our governor will be summoned to aid his brother to suppress the insurrection. No such summons ever comes and instead our treacherous governor, availing himself of his brother's distraction and grave problems, severs his allegiance to him and promptly proclaims himself king – the king of Gibel Tarik. We are horrified and the cruelties and tortures in the town intensify. Three weeks this terror lasts and then, strained to the very limits of our forbearance, exasperated and outraged, we cast all fear aside and rise against this evil. Goodly neighbours, friends and beggars, everyone explodes into a wave of fury as we rush up the hill towards the great square castle keep in which the new king and his son have locked themselves in abject panic. Our fury knows no bounds; with bare hands we tear at the doors and finally drag the simpering duo down to the square. Many are for slaughtering them there and then, but wiser counsels prevail and in the end, chained together like common criminals, we send them off to our sultan at Sebta.

Great is our consternation when we learn that the sultan has not had these two evil miscreants beheaded immediately as we had hoped. Then the news reach us of the horrible tortures which the betrayed sultan, in true family tradition, is devising and inflicting each day to avenge himself slowly and remorselessly on these treacherous traitors. The terrible revenge takes its toll and the word finally comes, the self-styled king of Gibel Tarik is dead and our misery is at an end.

May Allah grant us some peace at last.

The Raid

14

1433 AD

Only the glimmering stars speckled the intense blackness of the heavens on that moonless night, as the heavy creaking doors of the Atarazana, our boat yard, were slowly winched open. The sharp sound, whipping through the calm night, woke the seagulls dozing on the craggy rocks high above the sleeping town, but their raucous echoing cries served only to accentuate the stillness. We heaved and strained as we hauled the two long black galleys through the now-open doorway and onto the oily waters of the ebbing tide. Once afloat we jumped in and quickly started rowing. Soon we had left behind the high walls of the boat yard which sheltered our ships against storms and enemy alike. Silently the two vessels cut through the flat waters on their journey across the wide bay. Not a word was spoken. Every one knew his duty and set to it in total silence. We had all asked Allah for his blessing on this venture, our Jihad, our holy mission. We were engaged in righting a great wrong done to our people: recovering the fruits of our forefathers' labours. Was it not they who had cast the almadrabas in the Strait here all those years ago, long before those treacherous infidels so barbarously stole them from us and drove us from our homes and lands?

As we reached the head of the bay and set out through the Strait itself, only the soft rhythmic squeaking of the tholes and the muted laps of the dipping oars could be heard. Hugging the coast, we had to navigate carefully. These were dangerous waters and from the black shoreline we could see the darker fingers of jagged rocks reaching out towards us. Now and again we would hear the deep gurgling of whirlpools sucking at the surface, created by the swirling currents as the waters rushed through the narrows and out into the great ocean beyond. But we had been born and bred on these shores, this was our sea before the idolaters came and we knew all its hazards and dangers well. Far ahead in the black distance we could just make out the few flickering lights in the town of Tarifa. Our Tarifa, until it was ignominiously wrested from us, named after our great captain and conqueror, Tarif abu-Zarah, may Allah protect his memory. We had made sure that there were no vessels at this place on this day.

We gave the sleeping port a wide berth and sailed quickly along the coast. At the head of this long beach where the rolling sand dunes climb, steep hills jut out into the sea ending in a series of rocky reefs and it was in the lee of these that we finally hove to. Anchoring here, we sent men ashore to scour the immediate land and ensure that there was no one about. A party of us then made for the summit of the hills and, reaching the highest of these, we hid and waited for daybreak. As the sky lit up we could just make out the signalman on the adjoining hill; we kept a close watch on him. We were sure they would come. The rising tide, the soft wind and the strong currents were ideal. This was the beginning of spring when, fattened by their stay in the big ocean, they returned to our sea to spawn. If they did not come by noon we would have to return home immediately, for we could not risk being caught on this exposed coast.

It was shortly after sunrise when we saw them, almost at the same time as the signalman did. Far up the coast they came, a large blue-black stain ruffling the clear and calm waters and followed closely by a flurry of excited white seabirds. The signalman promptly raised his flags and from the beach to the north we saw the boats set off, laying out the long net as they went. As the pulsating mass neared this net it turned inland and the largest of the boats started to lay out another net, this was the real trap. Soon it had encircled the dark shoal and on the shore the hundreds of men started hauling in the ends. Even at this distance we could feel the excitement rising as the men closed the ring. Others in smaller boats pelted the waters with sticks and stones in order to keep the huge shoal within the trap.

Now the splashes of the captured giants could be seen churning the surface. As the water shallowed, the enclosure became a cauldron of hurtling fish; the panicking tuna dashing about and even leaping at the surface in vain attempts to elude the closing nets. The signal for the gaffing of the fish to commence was given.

The long hooked spikes were expertly sunk into the fat, silvery bellies of the racing tuna and sometimes their very momentum was used to haul them on to the beach. First the smaller ones were tackled and finally the large ones, veritable giants, some weighing more than five men, were hacked and hooked and hauled on to the sands. By then the water had become one huge pool of red frothing blood as frenzied half-naked men grappled with splashing wounded fish in that small square. We had sent for the galleys and soon we could see the sleek black vessels speeding out past the headland. By the time we reached the beach, the galleys had landed and most of the infidels had fled, leaving behind on the blood-splattered sands the blue and silver mounds of dying tunny.

We worked rapidly for we had to be well away before any counterattack from Tarifa could be organised or ships sent out from Cadiz to the rescue could reach us. It soon became apparent that there were far too many fish for us to take back. Once both vessels were full to the brim, the nets were slashed, the fishermen's boats were sunk and the few captured infidels secured. We realised that they would not be worth ransoming, but would serve well as rowers in our galleys.

By now the wind from the west had freshened, as we had known it would. We hoisted our sails and both boats surged forward rapidly. The white-topped waves racing after us and threatening to spill into the bows of the heavily-laden boats as the billowing sails strained against the ropes and propelled us swiftly forward. Soon in the distance we could see our home and refuge, the great white Gibel Tarik. We entered the bay confidently; there was no pursuit. The raid had gone as planned. In the well of both boats the tuna lay heaped, their barrel-shaped bodies now still – a veritable treasure. As the two galleys sped across that wide expanse of water, the sunlit Rock loomed larger and, as we got nearer, we could see the old heavy doors of the atarazana swinging open for us once more. As soon as we were within, they swung closed behind us and we were safe. Inside it seemed as if the whole town had come down to greet us. The tops of the walls were lined with all our cheering people. Behind them the flat, white roofs of the tiered houses climbed up the mountain to the towered castle and from the minarets, the muezzin's plaintive calls for the afternoon prayers drifted down. Thanks be to Allah for yet another success against the infidel usurpers of our lands.

High on the hill, across the isthmus, five horsemen stood and watched. The tallest of them, on the big grey mare, could be heard cursing as the black vessels disappeared into the walled town. Don Enrique de Guzman, count of Niebla, lord and master of all these lands and owner of all the almadrabas, the tuna traps in the Strait, fumed and cried for vengeance. He swore that one day he would storm those lofty walls and oust these Moorish raiders from their Rock lair. Three years after this raid, in one such doomed attempt, the boat in which he was endeavouring to land capsized and the count, clad in his heavy armour, was drowned at the foot of the great Rock. His corpse, recovered by the Moors from the sea, was hung in a basket from those very walls to warn others of the folly of attempting to capture the Rock.

Twenty-six years later, a lone horseman rode into the town of Tarifa with news that would end an era. He was a renegade Moor known to the Spaniards as Ali el Curro. The startling news he brought was that there were hardly any soldiers in Gibraltar to defend it. The governor and captains had gone to Malaga with most of the troops to fight in the civil war then raging with Granada. The mayor of Tarifa, after sending word to the grandees of these lands, the duke of Medina Sidonia and the count of Arcos, immediately set out with the small force that he could muster. He set up camp at the foot of the Rock and shortly after the first attacks were launched was able to confirm Ali el Curro's assertion that there were few defenders in the citadel. Indeed he soon learnt that the hapless and almost defenceless inhabitants were on the point of surrender, but he wished to wait for the noblemen to be present. When they did arrive there was much undignified squabbling between these men for the honour of accepting the capitulation and this was the start of a long-lasting feud between these titled families. In the end, Gibraltar was surrendered on 20th August 1462, the feast of St Bernard. The king of Castile, Enrique IV, quickly settled the claims of ownership of the Rock by the wrangling noblemen by promptly making it part of his own kingdom. In this rather ignominious way the almost continuous seven hundred and fifty years of Moorish rule of Gibraltar finally came to an end. Don Juan de Guzman, now duke of Medina Sidonia and son of Don Enrique, was at last able to recover his father's remains from the basket which still hung from the towering walls.

Los Conversos

15

1474 AD

At the foot of the great Rock the small windswept town, snuggling beneath the grey castle keep and enclosed within its high walls, was empty. The expulsion of its Christian citizens, few as they were, had not been easy, but the duke's orders had been explicit. The town must be vacated before the converts arrived. Only a small garrison remained. Owners of property would be allowed to return within a few days to negotiate the sale of their houses with the new arrivals.

Forty kilometres away the caravan of exhausted refugees had just passed Tarifa and was commencing the struggle up the narrow mountain road leading to Algeciras. Earlier they had received the sad news that pirates had attacked those that had opted to go by sea and many had perished. Was this nightmare ever to end? They themselves had guarded against any such eventuality by forming their own militia and the good duke had also provided a small contingent of soldiers. As they topped the pass of El Bujeo they got their first view of Gibraltar. A grey, white and green mountain rising from the sea and jutting out from the coast at the far end of a wide bay. It looked almost like an island, but they could just make out the narrow strip of sand that connected it to the mainland. A magnificent sight, the great Rock with wisps of feathery clouds streaming towards them from its crest seemed to beckon. Could this be their longed-for haven? Would they be safe from their tormentors here at last?

It took them another two days to round the bay and arrive at the town gates. There followed much squabbling over houses and building plots and then the bargaining with the previous owners. When their leader and new mayor, Don Pedro de Herrera, started appointing the various officers to run the town, there was more trouble, especially amongst the group that had come from Seville who felt they were being ignored. Many of these eventually decided to return to their homes. Of course they had not suffered half as much as those from Cordoba. For the latter there was no question of returning. They had to make the best of their new situation.

How could they forget the burning of their homes, the looting, the rapes and beatings and killings? Once they had dared to hope that by giving up their Jewish faith and converting to Christianity they would be safe, but this had not been so. Instead, branded permanently as 'Los Conversos', the converts, or even worse as 'marranos' (pigs), the validity of their conversions was forever in doubt by many because these had been obtained through fear after the dreadful pogroms eighty years earlier. They were constantly harassed and the slightest incident, real or imaginary, would rapidly lead to yet another attack on them and their property. They were considered different and the fact that they were educated and very capable, some holding high posts in the courts of the nobles, and were prosperous, did not help. They would always be the targets of bigotry, hatred, envy and just pure greed. Following a particularly vicious uprising against them in which many had perished, they had fled to Seville only to find the same hostility there.

After many attempts, their leader Don Pedro had at last managed to convince the duke of Medina Sidonia, Enrique de Guzman, the seigneur of these lands, to let them settle in the fortress town of Gibraltar which the king had finally ceded to the duke five years earlier. Under the agreement the conversos would pay for most of the cost of garrisoning the town for the first two years and a nominal fee thereafter. As the duke was empowered by the king to levy a tax on the people of Seville for the upkeep of this garrison, it meant that he would actually be pocketing a considerable sum for those two years. The duke, after much deliberation and no doubt further sweetening of the palm, had finally agreed. By this means he was also getting rid of the present Christian population of Gibraltar whom he suspected of wanting to petition the king for their town to revert to the crown of Castile.

The converts had in effect bought Gibraltar and hoped to make it a home for themselves and their people. A secure and safe haven at last, where in time they might even be able to practise their true faith without fear or hindrance.

Eventually the initial problems were solved and the settlers became a close-knit community. They repaired and strengthened the city walls and with difficulty maintained and paid for their garrisoning. They quickly established trading links with both the adjoining Spanish ports along the coast and the Moorish ones across the Strait. Soon the two years of payments would be up and they could look forward to a prosperous and safe future.

In the meantime, in yet another dynastic quarrel amongst the new kingdoms on the Iberian peninsula, Portugal was at war with Castile. The dispute centred on the legitimacy of the Infanta Juana, daughter of the late king of Castile and known spuriously as La Beltraneja. This king was considered to have been impotent and the suspected father was his favourite and former governor of Gibraltar, Beltran de la Cueva. At this time the enclave of Ceuta, on the African coast across the Strait, was a Portuguese colony. In Gibraltar, Don Pedro, with his knowledge of the poor defensive conditions in Ceuta garnered through his trading connections with that port, urged Don Enrique to attack it. As a loyal vassal he would give whatever support was required. Eventually the duke agreed and sent a fleet to assault and lay siege to Ceuta. This was no more than a half-hearted attempt and a few months later the duke himself set out from Seville with a large body of cavalry to drive home the attack. Before crossing the Strait he visited Gibraltar.

That day the whole town was down at La Barcina to greet their great benefactor, with the garrison on parade and Don Pedro at their head. As the duke and his entourage came through the city gate the mayor stepped forward to greet his lord. It was at this moment that he was ignominiously set upon and taken prisoner. His people looked on in bewilderment and fear. In that one instant they realised that their dream had been shattered. A proclamation was then read out. The duke begged forgiveness of his sovereign for having granted a part of the kingdom entrusted to him to heretics who had betrayed his good faith by giving aid to the infidels across the Strait. Today he was righting this wrong and restoring Gibraltar to true Christianity. Needless to say there was no mention of the deal or of the fact that the two years of payments had just elapsed.

History does not tell us what became of Don Pedro. As for his people, they were given a few days in which to abandon the city. Now penniless and destitute, they had nowhere else to flee to. A few sailed across the Strait to the Moorish kingdom there and others went to the Moorish kingdom in Granada, but the majority of them reluctantly decided to go back to the only land they knew, where they had been born, the land of their ancestors. Maybe now that they had nothing, no one would envy them and they would be left in peace.

They were wrong. A few years later the grand inquisitor, the Dominican Tomás de Torquemada and the Holy Office arrived in Cordoba and the burnings began.

The Corsairs

16

1540 AD

The land gates were just about to be closed on that blustery autumn evening when the horseman was spotted galloping across the sands. They waited until they were in, the slavering horse and the excited rider. That afternoon a corsair fleet of sixteen galleys, probably from their lair in Algiers, had been sighted off Malaga heading southwards. The warning had been relayed down the almenaras, the watchtowers that lined this dangerous coastline. From each tower a horseman would carry the message to the next and to all the coastal villages and towns in-between. Now the rider from the last tower up the coast had reached Gibraltar. The news swept quickly through the sleepy town, but the governor was away tending his vines across the isthmus, as were many of the townsmen. Those left in the town thought that Gibraltar was too small and insignificant for such a fleet and everyone agreed that they were probably on their way out into the Atlantic headed for richer prizes such as Cadiz. So, apart from setting up a few sentries along the coast, nothing was done and another horseman was dispatched on to Tarifa to relay the warning.

On the following morning, Juan was up before sunrise to go to his vineyard. The rains were due to start at any moment and he had to get as many of his grapes in as possible before then. Soon he was joined by many of the other farmers as they crossed the isthmus to their farms beyond, confident that the corsairs would not attack. Even his wife Maria was going out to pick the fruit, he needed all the help he could get. There would be no one left at home, for despite six years of marriage there were no children. It was his one great sadness. He was a simple man; all he really knew about was growing grapes. It had remained a source of wonder to him that Maria, the loveliest girl from Villa Vieja, had consented to marry him, a small vinegrower from La Turba outside the inner city walls with few prospects. Over the years he had tried everything, consulted the priest, the curandera, anyone who he thought could help, but to no avail. They had no children.

Just before dawn two young boys had slipped out through the city gates to gather mussels in the small bays at the southern end of the Rock. On arrival they found the corsairs' galleys anchored there and the Moors already disembarking. They rushed back into the town sounding the alarm, but by then most of the farmers had left for their lands at the head of the bay. After capturing the sentries and sacking the hermitage of Our Lady of Europe at the far end of the Rock, the Moors turned towards the town itself. The few soldiers in the garrison soon realised that it would be futile to try to defend the long wall to the south of the town, there just weren't enough of them. In any case the wall itself was in a poor state of repair and parts were even fallen. Instead they retreated into the castle, locked themselves in and concentrated on defending this bastion.

When they heard the corsairs coming, some of the women and children who were left in the town sought shelter in the large church of Santa Maria la Coronada where a few brave men managed to fend off the marauding enemy. Many others fled up the hill towards the castle in a desperate effort to seek refuge there, only to find on reaching it that the gates were locked. Some of the defenders of the castle eventually succumbed to their piteous cries for help and opened a small side gate for them. In the terrorised scramble to get to safety that followed some were trampled to death and many others injured in the narrow passageways of the keep.

It was only after the raid that they learned that Moorish captives, who had escaped from a prison ship in the bay where they were being held for ransom, had told the corsairs about the poor state of the defences at Gibraltar and the lack of manpower. Indeed it had been one of these very same convicts, Caramani, who had persuaded the viceroy of Algiers and the governor there, the infamous Barbarossa, to mount this raid and it was Caramani himself who was now one of the leaders of the assault on the town.

Despite repeated attempts the corsairs were unable to break into the castle and, having ransacked much of the large neighbourhood of La Turba, turned their attention to the richer walled quarters of Villa Vieja and La Barcina, but here they were frustrated by the stiff resistance of a handful of resolute fighters. From the few prisoners they did manage to capture they learnt that the majority of the people had gone to their farms. Gathering as much plunder as they could and setting fire to many buildings, they boarded their ships again and made for the mouth of the first river at the head of the bay. It was there amidst the vineyards that Juan, on seeing the corsairs landing again, urged his wife to seek shelter within the large warehouses where the fermenting wine was kept. When the corsairs burst into these storerooms they captured many of the farm people who had sought refuge there. Amongst these was Maria. Juan had stayed behind to save what he could of his vineyard.

The Moors re-embarked with many prisoners. When Juan heard the terrible news he despaired; he knew he would never be able to raise the high ransom that would inevitably be sought. Sadly he realised that he would never see Maria again. The corsairs attempted to ransom the prisoners before leaving for their base in North Africa, but the sums demanded were well beyond the resources of the ransacked town. The defenders offered to collect the monies from the neighbouring towns, but after waiting for two days the corsairs, suspecting this to be a ploy to delay them in the bay until reinforcements arrived, sailed away.

The news of the attack had reached Cartagena and it was fortuitous that that very afternoon a squadron of the Spanish naval fleet arrived in port under Admiral Bernardino de Mendoza. They set off immediately in pursuit. Guessing that the Moorish raiders would be making for Algiers, the Admiral sailed straight for the African coast and lay in wait across their path in the sea of Alboran. Sure enough, the enemy fleet was sighted at first light and in the ensuing battle, all but one of the enemy ships were either sunk or captured. The corsairs' delay in the bay whilst they awaited the outcome of their ransom demands had been crucial and their greed had proved fatal. Fortunately the ship in which most of those captured at Gibraltar were imprisoned was taken intact.

One month later the captives from Gibraltar arrived back home. There was great jubilation. Juan was overjoyed. This proved to be the best year of his life. His wife, despite the trauma, had survived and returned safe and sound. He was able to get in all his grapes before the rains arrived and it had turned out to be a bumper crop. But best of all was when, three months after her return, Maria announced that she was pregnant at last.

Another five months went by before the boy was born. The old and sage neighbourhood midwife assured him that, though small and premature, it was a perfectly healthy baby. And so it was. Young Juanito grew up into a fine and lusty lad, much taller than his father, but with his mother's looks. He turned out to be their one and only child, but Juan, thanking God for his divine mercy, had a son and heir at last.

The King's Coach

17

1624 AD

The excitement in the town had been mounting throughout the past week. The king was coming. None of us had ever seen a king before. We were so thrilled as there were few events to brighten our lives in this bleak fortress town of ours. Even our elders were excited. I was particularly elated, as my mother was to let me wear my Communion dress on the day, the only real dress I had. All the boys from the vineyards and the farms, the boat builders, the fishermen, everyone would be there. I wanted to look my best.

Now here we were, all dressed up and standing atop the town's defence walls, peering northwards, waiting eagerly. We had been here since noon when we had been told he would come, but now, three hours later, there was no sign of the royal party. Under the hot summer sun our enthusiasm was flagging. Maybe he was not coming after all.

Then, just as we were losing hope, there was a sharp cry as far away beyond the flat land a yellow dust cloud could be seen getting steadily nearer. Soon we could make out the multi-coloured cavalrymen, their lances flashing in the sunlight, galloping towards us. Behind them came the coach pulled by six magnificent black horses, a coach as none had seen before. It glistened in the afternoon sun and seemed to be made entirely of gold. At the rear, more horsemen followed bearing the royal standards, flapping strongly in the breeze. A truly magnificent sight.

As they came nearer, the crowd grew evermore excited, but we kept silent for we had all been told to remain as quiet as possible until the moment when the royal coach entered the town when we were all to give a mighty cheer. Now as the tall cavalrymen, tilting their long lances forward, came through the city walls at the Landport gates and burst into La Barcina, everyone braced themselves for the appearance of the black horses pulling the golden coach. But there was nothing. We waited eagerly but no horse or coach, golden or otherwise, entered the sunlit Calleja. Our welcoming cheers remained unuttered. The cavalry horses came to a halt and turned back towards the town gates. There was confusion as soldiers rushed in and soon the news raced through the waiting crowds. The coach had got stuck in the gates and could not be dislodged.

It was quite a while before an agitated young man was seen emerging from the Landport opening, strutting out and obviously in none too good a temper. Quickly through the waiting crowd the message spread. This was he. This was the king. Belatedly we cheered, but it was not as we had all expected. The monarch strode ahead looking neither left nor right and was closely followed by a coterie of hurrying grandees. One of these we learnt was the duke of Medina Sidonia and behind them all, obviously very flustered, our own governor Don Luis Bravo.

Slowly the crowd dispersed. Everyone was disappointed. This was to have been such a glorious day. Our one chance to see and welcome our own King Philip. Wearily I climbed the steep hill on my way home. I knew that I was unlikely to get another opportunity to wear my lovely dress, now crumpled and soiled. My mother would probably unpick it all and keep the material for use sometime in the future. Maybe for my wedding dress, one day.

Despite the disappointment of the population of this tiny town, some good did come from this unfortunate fracas. The next day, when the king's minister, the Count-Duke Olivares, complained and reprimanded Don Luis for not having foreseen such an eventuality, the wily governor answered that the gates had been designed to keep the king's enemies out of his majesty's fortress and not to allow coaches to drive in. He seized the opportunity to ask again for funds to fortify the area, something he had been doing without success for some years now. He knew that during the whole affray the young monarch had had ample time to see for himself the sorry state of the fortifications. There soon followed major reconstruction of all the northern defences.

Exodus

18

1704 AD

My uncle had a small farm beyond the red sands. Small, but in that fertile area very productive. Every Sunday after Mass, we, that is my brother and sisters, and there were seven of us, would hike out there to spend the day. It was the highlight of our week. To us it was a magical place full of all kinds of animals from long-bearded billy goats to small furry rabbits. The old man waged an ongoing battle with the rock apes, which repeatedly raided his fruit trees, and also set traps for the foxes that now and again made off with one of his chickens. We played on the farm and the surrounding slopes until we were worn out. In the evening we would return home laden with farm produce. I can remember walking home through the narrow streets and then up the steep ramps after these hectic days, keen to get home and lay all the goods before my mother. She would sell most of them from the tiny shop at the front of the house; this was our only source of income. After my father's sudden death she had donned the traditional widow's black and hardly ever left the house and, when not serving behind the counter, was continuously tidying and cleaning it. The house was her pride and joy. That, and cooking for all of us. Even in her later years she would allow no one near the kitchen when she was preparing a meal.

Every morning at dawn my brother and I woke first, for we were altar boys down at the big church of Santa Maria la Coronada. We would clamber over our sleeping sisters and look out of the window on to that lovely bay. It was on one such morning in the middle of a long hot summer that we saw them. Lots and lots of beautiful ships. Our sisters were soon also fully awake and staring out at this wonderful sight. It was then that we heard the commotion in the street. Men, our neighbours, were rushing up the ramp and urging their families out of the houses.

Many were even carrying some of their belongings. Soon our mother was downstairs trying to find out what all the fuss was about. It seemed that we were about to be attacked by these ships. The Austrian pretender Carlos had sent this troops to take over the fortress of Gibraltar. This fleet of foreign ships was helping him.

Many of our neighbours were leaving for the south, as far away as possible from the bombardment that could start at any moment. My mother would not budge. She would stay at her house, no matter what, shelter her children at the back and await the outcome. She did not really understand politics and her only concern was for her home and family.

We spent most of that day at the window watching the tall war ships manoeuvring into position, hoping our own fleet would come and we would see a great sea battle. Now and again someone would run up the ramp shouting that the invading soldiers would be marching in at any moment, or that our army was coming to save us. No one knew what was really happening. It was early the following morning that we saw the first white puffs of smoke billow out of the ships, followed quickly by loud bangs. The gun firing had started, but fortunately for us the majority of the shells fell on the mole and on the lower town in La Barcina. We were relatively safe up here. It was all terribly exciting. Later some of the shells were to fall much nearer. Still my mother refused to leave. Our ramp and the adjoining street were now practically deserted. Shortly after this my uncle the farmer, my mother's brother, arrived. He was the only one my mother would listen to. At last we were leaving, he had persuaded her for our sakes, especially when he told her that some of the invaders were the dreaded heretic Britons.

Carrying a few possessions each, mainly bedding and food, we ran down the ramp. Our uncle was leading us to the deep gorges to the south beyond the bays. He assured us we would be safe there until the enemy fleet was driven off. People were streaming out in the same direction and I spotted and waved at some of my friends. Through the main street of La Turba we hurried, until we reached the long wall that runs down from the top of the Rock. Here we came upon a large crowd. The gates had been closed against the invading army. Only when the guards realised that the crowd was beginning to panic did they agree to open the gates just long enough for us to get out.

It was as we were running past the red sands, near my uncle's farm that we met them. Troops of tall ferocious looking soldiers rushing towards us. At that moment the excitement ended for us youngsters and we were overcome with fear. I can still recall my mother standing in front of all of us wielding a wooden hayfork defending us like a wildcat. A couple of my sisters were old enough to cause her great concern and we could already hear the screams coming from those further up the hill. Fortunately, their captain arrived and leaving some soldiers behind to guard us, took the rest towards the town, their real target. We would be used as one of the pawns to convince our governor, Don Diego, to surrender the fortress.

Sadly we watched as part of our beloved town went up in flames. The commotion was unbelievable; the gunfire from the ships, the screams and shouts of battle, the crackling of the flames, and closer to us the woeful cries of the women amongst us. When it was all over we were herded back into the town. Surprisingly our house was intact, but when we got inside we saw that it had been ransacked. Our meagre possessions had either been smashed or taken. As soon as my mother stepped over the threshold she set to and started making the place habitable for the family again.

The next day we learnt that the fortress had been surrendered and we were given the option to leave or stay under the rule of the pretender Carlos. We were allowed three days in which to decide. My mother was adamant. We would stay in our house come what may. But next morning we saw most of our neighbours leaving and shortly after this my uncle arrived and once again persuaded her to leave. These northern invaders were practically all Protestants and included many Britons. They had committed many atrocities, rape and looting and had also pillaged the churches. Even the much-revered statue of the Virgin of Europe in the shrine at the southern tip of the Rock had not been spared. What else could one expect from these heretics? In any case he argued, it would only be for a short time for soon King Philip would come with loyal troops and restore us to our home.

And so it was that on the following morning shortly after daybreak, taking as many of our belongings as we could, we joined the column of refugees on the long trek. Down through the ruins of La Barcina we struggled. Here many of the buildings had been destroyed and some were still smouldering. The streets were lined with armed soldiers shouting and jeering at us in a foreign language as we passed. At the Landport gate Father Juan was waiting to bless all those who were leaving. Sorrowfully he told us that he would miss us at Mass each morning. He was staying behind to try and look after his beloved church. He said he was determined to stay there night and day if necessary to prevent a repetition of what had happened at the shrine.

As the long line of refugees wound its way across the sandy isthmus, we all looked back at our precious Rock, looming above us and receding as the day wore on, wondering sadly when we would see our homes again. All that is except my mother, who refused to look back but set her face resolutely towards the distant hills and walked steadfastly on.

That was a long time ago now, but on most evenings thereafter, even when she was a very old woman, after serving us our supper, our mother would climb slowly up to the flat roof of the house. There she would sit saying her rosary, staring south at the distant Rock that she had always considered her true home. From up here at San Roque, where we had settled all those years ago, it was a truly magnificent view. The Rock rises proudly from the surrounding sea. It appears to have been set there purposely to taunt us. When it was getting dark I or one of my sisters would come and coax her down. We could always tell that she had been crying. To the very end she clung to the hope that the king would come again with his army and throw those perfidious, heretic English out of her beloved Gibraltar and restore her to the home where she had been born and the Rock where all her ancestors lay buried. She waited in vain for she died and it never happened.

The Whirligig

19

1782 AD

I was nine years old when I saw my mother in the whirligig. She had not come home all day and we had not eaten a thing since breakfast. We were frightened and apprehensive and in the late afternoon, leaving my four little sisters in the one room we all shared, I ventured down into the town. It was as I turned the corner in the lane that goes by the old mill that I saw the crowd. A motley collection of ruffians, shouting and teasing. The children amongst them were throwing scraps of garbage at the cage. And there inside the cage was my mother, clad in the skimpy dress in which she had left home that morning, now besmirched with filth. Her head hung low, but I could see that she was crying as she went round and round. I was thankful that her eyes were closed for I did not want her to see that I was there. It was dreadful. There was nothing I could do to help her and, holding back my own tears, I ran on down the lane, away from this painful scene, until I reached the large city square. Here I found a bigger crowd shouting and swearing. I squeezed and squirmed my way through to the centre and finally saw what the commotion was all about. Two men, stripped to the waist, were strung up on the whipping posts and were in the process of being lashed, their backs were already streaming with blood. Between the sharp sounds of the lash and the screaming of the victims, I learnt from the bystanders' shouts what had really happened.

These two soldiers, for such they were, had been stealing stores from the military compound and giving them to my mother. A heinous crime in this time of siege. A horrible sense of guilt and fear gripped me for, had I not partaken of these very same goods? Many years later I understood what my mother had been required to give in return.

From that day on we were shunned by all our neighbours in the patio where we lived. Eventually we had to move out. We wandered through the almost deserted town. Most of the people had fled to the south away from the gunfire. Eventually we set up a home of sorts in one of the abandoned bombed-out houses which littered the lower town. Fortunately this was towards the end of the siege and there were fewer heavy bombardments. I remember being constantly hungry; the search for enough food was our only daily concern.

At daybreak each morning we would sally forth. My mother would station my sisters outside the kitchens of the big army barracks, with instructions to beg for anything. They were never very successful, they were young and there were so many others. I suspect that much of what they did get was quickly snatched from them. They probably gulped down anything they got before it was taken. She herself then went off to forage for whatever she could pick up and I was left to my own devices.

Before the siege started I had been a goatherd on the slopes above the town, but all the goats had been eaten long ago. Now I scoured the ruined town, begging from the many soldiers, stealing from those that were drunk and scavenging everywhere. If there had been a bombardment the previous night, I would search the bombed-out buildings for any scraps, anything that was edible. There were many of us, men, women and children, all searching frantically. Any food stores in the bombed-out houses were quickly commandeered by the military, but a dead cat or even a rat was a great find, and there would be much fighting over these. You had to be sharp and quick on your feet. If you got caught in any of these ventures you were liable to get a sound beating and I had received many, but we were all starving and desperate. Our one distraction was climbing the slopes when there was a battle going on and watching the gunfire, the burning and sinking ships. From up there you could even hear the screams and cries of battle, but lately things had quietened down. It was from this vantage-point that we would first spot any vessel with fresh supplies that managed to get through the enemy cordon and then everyone would rush down to the moles.

I can still recall the big parade on St George's Day on the red sands, which marked the end of this horrible siege. It was a wonderful event with marching soldiers and massed bands. Out in front rode our victorious Governor Elliot in his plumed hat and red coat, mounted on the only horse in the parade. This horse, a beautiful grey Andalusian, had been given to him when peace was declared by the duc de Crillon, commander of the besieging forces

After this our lives changed and slowly, over the years, life on this great Rock became much better, especially after the victory at Trafalgar and Napoleon's defeat. The town prospered. My poor mother did not live much longer to enjoy this, she died young, no doubt exhausted by her struggle to bring us up in such dire times. The only daughter of a Portuguese fisherman, she had taken up with a soldier when she was still practically a girl and this soldier, my father, promptly abandoned us when his regiment was posted elsewhere.

Two of my sisters were taken in the fevers of 1804, but those who are left have a better life. My eldest sister, Ethel, married into one of the Genoese families living at the head of Waterport Street that are involved in the tobacco trade and is quite well off. My youngest sister, Mary, married a soldier who, unlike my own father, has stuck by her and they live happily in one of the army married quarters on the upper Rock. As for me, I married a Spanish girl from across the border; we have raised our own family and live well on my wages from a ship chandler in the bustling Irish Town. The whole place is thriving. A lot of rebuilding has been carried out and much has changed. Even the whirligig has been taken down enabling me to go through the twisting Mill Lane again without recalling those horrible times.

Winged Death

20

1828 AD

The day's washing was finished and the sagging clothes lines, strung across the length of the cobbled patio, were festooned with the brilliant whites of the early morning labours. The small washhouse at the far end lay quiet and empty in the afternoon shade. Over now was the boisterous banter of the washerwomen and all that could be heard was a faint humming at the rear where the wooden barrel halves were lined up, laden with stagnant rainwater, stored for future washes. It was too dark to see the tiny wriggling larvae within, but now and again the small comma-shaped pupae interrupted the flat sheen of the water as they bounced up towards the surface. Occasionally one lingered there awhile and then, as if by magic, the brittle skin along its back split and from it emerged a sticky, spindly fly. For a few seconds it floated precariously on its long legs and then the transformation began. Two tiny crumpled appendages on its back filled out, forming long sinuous veined wings and the body darkened and became striated in black and white colours, making it one of the most attractive of mosquitoes. Here in these dark, hot recesses, reminiscent of those faraway jungles where they had originated, they found the pools of limpid, woody water in which they thrived. A frolic of humming and buzzing ensued, as the males with their plumed antennae endeavoured to mate with the larger females. Then, duly fertilised, the females flew off into the night in search of fresh blood, essential if they were to produce eggs.

That evening in the waning light of the dying day, the *Dygden*, battered and bruised, sailed into the bay. A Swedish brig of dubious repute, she had left Havana forty-seven days earlier with a cargo of sugar and logwood and had weathered a stormy crossing. As soon as the port authorities learnt that there had been a number of deaths on board, she was placed in quarantine. Later though, her captain managed to convince the officials that these fatalities were due to the bad conditions during the crossing and she was allowed to come alongside. Her crew swarmed ashore and promptly made for the famed wineshops of Waterport Street. Then, their thirst quenched, they sought to assuage other cravings sharpened by their long and arduous sea voyage. They soon made their way up the hill to the renowned narrow lanes where brightly dressed ladies welcomed them with open arms. Most of them spent the night there and it was thus, somnolent in the arms of Venus, that the female mosquitoes, with cravings of their own, found them. The virus, which these seamen had inadvertently transported across the Atlantic, was about to be disseminated by these blood-sucking vectors amongst the unsuspecting inhabitants of this busy seaport.

Three weeks later, the bustling, thriving town had been transformed into a veritable inferno. The air was acrid with the stench of rotting flesh and the smell of burning as large fires blazed night and day at the bottom of the ramps and steps. Here the property of all those living in houses where the disease had struck was burnt in a desperate effort to stem the spread of the dreadful scourge. Many, trying to save their belongings, would hide their dead relatives. Others, desperate to rid their families of contagion, would take their dead down to the Spanish church, whilst those without strength would just lay them out on their doorsteps. In some households whole families lay dead or stricken by the terrible affliction. Daily the creaking death carts roamed the almost deserted streets, picking up the diseased yellowed corpses and transporting them out beyond the city walls, to be dumped into huge burial pits dug by weary soldiers.

Those who could remember the last terrible epidemic just over twenty years earlier, which had killed half the population, soon fled to the camps being set up on the isthmus. These were said to be miraculously free of the disease. Many of the soldiers were also quartered on the isthmus and others at Windmill Hill, whilst the governor with his family and servants moved to Governor's Cottage behind the Rock. The port was closed and the Spanish authorities sealed all access to the fortress. Fortunately the Spaniards delivered food across the narrow isthmus in a macabre arrangement whereby the food was deposited half way across. Merchants from the fortress would then sally forth to collect it and would in turn leave money, deposited in pails of vinegar. Thus any physical contact was avoided.

In the town all efforts to eradicate or even contain the terrible disease proved useless in stemming its onslaught. Experts from England and France came to study and try to discover cures for this malaise as they had done during the previous epidemic. They recorded in detail the terrible symptoms of the disease which culminated in most cases in the yellow pigmentation of the skin of the victims. They noted how those who had contracted the disease and survived appeared to be immune to it from then on. They observed that most cases seemed to be concentrated in the heavily built-up town, whilst the open spaces like the Neutral Ground and Windmill Hill were relatively free from the disease. This led some to suspect the overcrowding or bad drainage. Many theories were proposed and all sorts of remedies tried, but nothing seemed to stop the progress of the disease in the hapless victims and over half of them died. Very few families were unaffected by the scourge and the survivors were left, weak and impoverished, to reconstruct their shattered lives in the devastated town.

Who would have thought then that the tiny mosquitoes humming away through the night and at worst considered a seasonal nuisance, were the stealthy purveyors of doom? It was not until thousands had been infected and the onset of winter stopped the mosquitoes breeding that the epidemic abated. Almost a hundred years were to elapse before the culprit was finally identified and not until 1932 was immunisation to become available.

Now in the old washhouse at the end of the cobbled patio the lone female mosquito flies desperately around. Gone are the wooden half barrels with their warm, soft rainwater, replaced by metal galvanised tubs filled with cold, clear tap water. In the end, tiring of her hapless search she lays her tiny egg floats on the surface of the water in one of these. The water is the wrong temperature or maybe not chemically suitable. They never hatch.

The last recorded finding of the larvae of the yellow fever mosquito in Gibraltar was in 1951.

Days of Empire

21

1880 AD

The boy stood by the rain-splashed window staring out into the relentless drizzle of a grey Lancashire evening. Yet another cold and miserable day: there had been no playing in the garden again. It had been this way for the whole week, but as it turned out, today would be different, this was the day when his father came home with the exciting news that he was to be posted overseas. The boy was not quite sure what this would mean and watched his mother closely for her reaction; she seemed to greet the news with some dismay. His father was a captain with the Royal Welch Fusiliers and his regiment was to be stationed in some outpost of the vast British Empire. They were to be told on the following day, but there were rumours of far-off exotic places, India, Australia or even Hong Kong.

That night his mother came to his bedside with a large atlas and showed him on the very first pages a world map of the Empire, their Empire. She explained that all those red patches scattered all over the pages were theirs and their home for the next few years could be on any one of them. Henceforth the boy would love to open this atlas and his heart would swell with pride as he surveyed for the umpteenth time the expanse of reds scattered throughout the double pages.

Wherever it was, it was almost certain to be sunnier, his father had said, probably by way of encouragement, but the boy was apprehensive. He had just started at a new school; did this mean that he would have to leave all his new-found friends?

The following day his father came with the dispatch, it was to be the Rock of Gibraltar. Quickly the excited boy rushed for the atlas and asked his father to show him where it was. He was somewhat disappointed; it was just a very small red dot at the base of a large square piece of land. It did not look very impressive. There would be no tigers or elephants, not even kangaroos. He was not aware of this at the time, but fate had just intervened and changed the whole course of his future.

Two months elapsed before they actually set sail, and during this time his father regaled him with stories of the famous fortress that was to be their home. Gibraltar, the strongest fortress in the world, the many sieges it had withstood in its turbulent history, the great sea battles fought nearby, including the most famous of all, Trafalgar.

The sturdy P & O steam packet *Cathay* pitched and tossed as they crossed the infamous Bay of Biscay. The boy had a terrible voyage; he was seasick for the entire journey. Then one morning he woke up to a great stillness. Excitedly he rushed up on deck. There it was, a huge great Rock rearing up above them resplendent in the blazing sunshine. The blue sea between them and the shore was alive with all manner of craft. Close in, their ship was encircled by small boats, the occupants of which, in a cacophony of strange tongues, were busy trying to sell their multicoloured wares to those passengers who would be going on to India and beyond. Further out larger boats plied to and from other ships bound for Spain, Italy, Africa, India and the Americas.

Once ashore they were taken through the huge city gates and up to the very centre of the lively town. Here again they were greeted by a veritable medley of cries, strange languages and bright colours, men in turbans, skullcaps, djellabahs, and soldiers everywhere, constantly marching up and down in their red coats and other colourful uniforms. Here and there tall pyramids of black round cannon balls could be seen. From all the vantagepoints atop the high stone seawalls, upon the many massive batteries and on the Rock itself, the menacing black muzzles of hundreds of guns pointed out to sea. That evening, when they had reached their house and settled in, he stood by the window in his new bedroom looking out at that wondrous bay, listening to the trumpet calls as the sun set and to the 'All's Well' of the sentinels far and near until late into the night. It was all fascinating and for the rest of his life he always felt that he had lost his heart to Gibraltar on that very first day.

They settled down to a life of luxury on the Rock. A beautiful house surrounded by verandas and exotic gardens halfway up the Rock with spectacular views of Spain and, across the Strait, the serrated ranges of the dark mountains of Africa. There were Spanish maids and Gibraltarian gardeners and farriers to care to their every need. Socially his parents were in a constant whirl of parties and dinners, even fox hunting in neighbouring Spain with the famous Calpe Hunt. For him there was the special services school with outings into the surrounding wild countryside, thrilling parades, band concerts, gymkhanas at the local racecourse, sailing in the bay. An idyllic life, but despite all of this he was lonely. There were few boys of his own age to play with and of course to his parents it would be unthinkable that he should mingle with the local children. Instead he spent hours looking out to sea.

He soon learnt to recognise all the major shipping lines. The P & O packet steamers with their outward and homeward bound boats every Tuesday seemed to set the rhythm of this very busy port. There were British vessels bound for South and East Africa and others, like the P & Os, to India, the Far East and Australia, all serving the far-flung outposts of Empire. Vessels from other nations also came in, Italian, American, Spanish, Swedish, all bound for foreign ports within the Mediterranean or to northern Europe or even out across the ocean to North and South America. Smaller local boats crossed the Strait to the North African ports of Tangier, Ceuta and Casablanca, the list was endless. Most thrilling of all though were the Royal Navy warships, bristling with guns and festooned with flags and always granted pride of place within the harbour, especially the big battleships like the *Bellerophon* and the *Agincourt*. This last, his father told him, had actually gone aground on the infamous Pearl Rock. This treacherous reef, which had claimed many a good ship, lay just below the surface off the Spanish headland they could see from their veranda right across the bay. It had happened just a few years before they arrived. For three days the Navy had struggled to refloat her. In the end they had brought in another battleship to pull her off.

When there was little activity he would amuse himself in the garden, fighting the Pathans of India until he was ready to drop, but it was no real fun on his own. How he wished he could have someone to play with. Then, one day their gardener, Joseph, brought his young daughter Rosie to the garden. They played all that afternoon and after that she came often and they became close friends. Almost a year went by before his mother, surfacing momentarily from her social rounds, noticed his growing infatuation with the girl and promptly brought matters to a head by forbidding the gardener from bringing her again. The boy was devastated and his futile attempts at seeing the girl only led to poor Joseph's dismissal.

He was a teenager before he saw her again. He had a bit more freedom now and at school lunchtime he could slip down into the town. There, amidst the bustling life of the crowded ramps full of chattering women, he would meet her. Surrounded by the greengrocers from Spain with their little donkey carts bursting with colourful fruits and vegetables, the fishmongers with their panniers full of freshly caught silvery fish, their hawking cries melding with the flutes of the tinkers and the aromas of ambulant sellers of sweets, their friendship blossomed.

Fate now intervened again to put an end to all of this. His father was to be posted back to England. He never did find out whether his father had requested this posting because of his liaison with a local girl. Maybe the Colonial Authorities themselves, who frowned on such close contacts with the natives, particularly among the officers and their kin, had contrived it. The result was that on one balmy hot August evening they boarded the tender that was taking the passengers to the packet steamer on her way back to England anchored out in the bay. It was a traumatic moment for the youngster and as the little ship left the pier he thought he caught a glimpse of a young girl lurking in the shadows on the wharf. She had come to say goodbye.

I did not return until twenty years later. I had followed the family tradition and joined my father's regiment and in this period saw much of this great empire of ours. Finally I managed to get a posting back to the Rock, eventually retired here and have stayed on ever since. Today I live at the top of one of those lively ramps I used to love so much as a youth. They all call me 'El Ingles' here, for in all these years I have never been able to master the local patois, a mixture of Spanish and English, called Llanito. Now, in the twilight of my life, I sit again in the evenings on my veranda and watch the ships sailing in and out of this splendid bay. There are still the P & Os of yesteryear and all the other vessels sailing to distant ports, but it is the Navy fleets that now dominate the bay. First the sleek destroyers speed quickly in followed by the heavier cruisers and then the mighty battle ships with their big guns steam proudly into port. They cram into the harbour until there is no more space left and overflow into the bay, filling up the whole area in a splendid pageant of majestic power.

As the sun goes down, Rosie comes and sits by me and together we look on as the red orb sets the sea ablaze with colour before it dips behind the hills above Algeciras and the boom of the sunset gun signals the end of another day.

Civil War

22

1936 AD

Everyone said that this was going to be the best fair yet and that there would be many brand new rides. We were all so very excited. Finally the day arrived and we set off, fingering in anticipation the few coins our father had given us to enjoy ourselves. The raucous noise in the fair was, as it always is in these festivals, overpowering. To the usual blaring of klaxons, sirens and countless growling machines was added the strident sounds from dozens of loudspeakers all screaming out their flamenco songs. In the background the murmur of thousands of people could be heard, interspersed by the shrieks and shouts of excitement of those on the rides. The multiple coloured lights, the heady smells of cooking foods and sweets and the all-encompassing hazy dust made for the total atmosphere of euphoria and we were soon immersed in this intoxicating tumult.

We were sitting in the brightly-coloured cart of one of the new rides, waiting apprehensively for it to start on its whirling journey, when we heard the first bangs. Everyone thought that some fool had set off the fireworks before the allotted time, but as the explosions increased in tempo and volume, the excitement turned to fear and suddenly everything seemed to come momentarily to a standstill and then people started screaming and rushing off. We soon joined the panicking crowds running for home down darkened lanes. As we turned towards our own home we could see the lucky ones, the Llanitos, the Gibraltarians, continuing on down the lane towards the shelter of their Rock haven.

My mother's relief when she found on reaching home that my father was there was unbounded. At the local hospital, where he was a senior nurse, he was the workers' union representative and a well-known firebrand. In the distance the firing could be heard, whilst far away at the fairground everything had gone quiet, even the lights had gone off. All that night we stayed up behind locked doors waiting and watching furtively through narrow window slats, but there was no movement in our lane.

The following morning my father tried to calm my mother, he was not unduly concerned himself and was sure that things would settle down as they had done on a number of occasions before. My mother was not to be calmed, especially when she heard the rumours in the neighbourhood of the brutality of the crimes being committed by the rebels. She became hysterical when she learnt that some of the doctors at the hospital had been taken out and summarily shot, but her urgent pleas for my father to flee were to no avail, he would not leave us. All my mother managed to get him to do was to stay indoors until everything was over.

It was on the second day that they came for him. At dawn there was a violent banging on the door and when my mother tentatively opened it was torn aside by rough soldiers who burst into their bedroom and unceremoniously dragged my father out with them, hitting him as they went and calling him a Red traitor. In a few moments he was gone and we were left crying and bewildered. The only consolation in my mother's grief was that she had insisted that my father go to bed fully clothed during all this trouble. She did not want him dragged out into the street in his nightclothes.

We were unable to find out what was happening to him, not even where he was being kept. There was chaos everywhere. Then, two days later, just as suddenly as he had been taken, he was back. Bald, battered and bruised from many beatings. His hair had all been shaved off. What really horrified me though was when he told us that he had been forced to drink a whole glass of castor oil. Remembering the terrible ordeal I went through when I was given just a spoonful of this vile stuff, I shuddered with disgust.

As the days went by the situation became more dangerous, but what finally convinced my father that we should try to leave was the presence of the dreaded Moorish troops. Now though, it was impossible to get across the isthmus into Gibraltar, the obvious place to flee to. Desperately he searched for ways to get us all away from the anarchy in the country, but to no avail, no one wanted to risk the wrath of the merciless Nationalist soldiers and their followers by helping suspects to escape. He had practically given up hope when, very late one night, there was a knock on our door. We froze, but it was only a frightened old fisherman who had spent a long time critically ill at the hospital and was grateful for my father's care of him. He just came in to say that the following night he would leave his oars inside his boat on the levant beach and was quickly gone.

And so it was that on that moonless night we carefully made our way on to the beach. Down by the fence we could just make out the lights of Nationalist soldiers patrolling the frontier. With difficulty we managed to launch the boat that had fortunately been left near the waters edge and, as noiselessly as possible, rowed out into the darkness. It was just a short distance really though our great fear made it seem an interminable journey. Even in the darkness we could make out the imposing north face of the Rock rising vertically into the black sky. What a welcome sound that muffled crunch was as the boat's keel dug into the soft beach sand. Soon we were surrounded by people helping us to haul out the boat on to the Gibraltar seashore. We were safe.

There were policemen and soldiers amongst them and we were apprehensive, but they only wanted to check our papers. After this we were taken to a tented camp on what used to be the racecourse. My father had often brought me here as a youngster to watch the races. Gibraltar was full of refugees from the civil war in Spain, many without papers and most penniless. We stayed on in this camp and later moved into the town.

We lived in cramped conditions and my father managed to get the odd temporary job. It was not a comfortable life, but at least we were safe from the terror that was raging in our country just across the frontier. We grieved as we learnt of the ravages being committed by the Falangist mobs in our homeland. From the safety of the Rock we would sometimes see our warships in the Strait and now and again witness a sea battle or bombardment of the adjoining coasts.

Meanwhile the storm clouds were gathering over the rest of Europe and a full-scale war with Germany seemed imminent. In Gibraltar, the fortress was being prepared for the coming conflict. Amongst the civilian population, many of them our friends who had helped us in our hour of need, apprehension was growing as the situation worsened. Rumours about the possible evacuation of all the women and children abounded and people were fearful. Finally, when the Republicans were defeated and thousands were being executed, we realised we could not go back to our country and managed to get passages to England and left.

Thirty years later I was able to bring my father back to his homeland. Many of the refugees had been offered a pardon if they returned to Spain and I ascertained at the Spanish embassy in London that my father would be included in this amnesty.

As the plane circled Gibraltar in that wide sweep around the Rock to line up with the tiny airstrip, I tried to get my father interested in this truly spectacular view. He had eyes only for his home, the sprawling town that straddled the land at the base of the isthmus across the frontier, La Linea.

We should have had no trouble crossing that frontier into Spain, a mere couple of hundred yards from the airport. The guards were just waving people through after a very brief glance at their papers, but one of these guards, noticing my father's agitation, decided to take his passport in for close examination.

Their whole attitude changed immediately, the police were summoned and my stunned father was brusquely taken into custody. All my protests about the amnesty were ignored. Even the production of the letter from the Spanish embassy was disregarded and indeed I just barely managed to get back into Gibraltar myself.

The Spanish authorities refused to recognise the British passport he now held and it was only after the intervention of the British embassy at Madrid a week later that he was finally released and expelled from Spain once more.

He was a broken man after that and a further six years were to elapse before he was finally able to go back to his hometown. He would never trust the dictator Franco again; the man who had taken over his country so brutally, clung stubbornly to power, destroyed many of his friends and all of his dreams. He preferred to wait until the merciless tyrant was dead.

Unternehmen Felix

23

1940 AD

With a mighty hiss the train finally came to a halt. A cloud of steam promptly enveloped the whole station and into this a very dishevelled and plainly exhausted German stepped. He had been on the train for over twenty-two hours. During the last stages of the interminable journey from Madrid, an additional engine had been coupled on to enable the slow train to climb over the high mountains surrounding Ronda. In the end they were eight hours late.

As the smoke dispersed and he looked across the almost bare platform he beheld a wonderful sight. Beyond the town's rooftops, a glittering bay and on the far side a recumbent lion like mountain, his ultimate goal, the mighty Rock of Gibraltar. He was a major in the German army, commissioned with the task of overseeing the final groundwork here for Operation Felix, the capture of the British Fortress of Gibraltar.

He looked around him, for he was supposed to have been met by a Spanish army officer. He was, of course, dressed in civilian clothes, for this was a highly secret operation and he had assumed that the officer who would meet him would be likewise. They were to recognise each other by wearing a red carnation in their lapels so he was quite disconcerted when he was hailed loudly by a portly man in full army uniform, 'Major! Major!' It was a prelude to the kind of lackadaisical attitude he would have to contend with in these southern lands. They quickly got into a car and drove down through the port of Algeciras and as they did so he could not help wondering what would become of this town once the big guns in Gibraltar started firing.

He was driven to the very seafront. Here he was taken to a sumptuous villa, which was to be their headquarters. From the veranda they had a superb view of the Rock across the bay. It would serve as a constant reminder of their difficult mission.

He spent the next couple of weeks going over the plans for the proposed invasion of the Rock. The available spies and possible sabotage operations within the Fortress, the siting of gun batteries in the mountains behind Algeciras and around the bay, the pinpointing of the entrances to the many tunnels on the Rock on which these guns would concentrate their fire power, even the advisability of a reconnaissance by him of the Rock itself. He toured the countryside in the immediate vicinity until he found, in the valley leading to the hilltop town of Jimena, the ideal flat land suitable for the building of a temporary airstrip. He realised now that the prospect of bringing troops down on the Spanish trains was not feasible and the bulk of the forces would have to come down in motorised columns.

There were of course other German officers, all experts in their various fields, already here and they soon dissuaded him from visiting the Rock personally. He had no problem with the language for he spoke Spanish well, having served with the Condor Legion here during the Civil War. The idea had been for him to mingle with the thousands of dockyard workers who entered Gibraltar every day, but security within the fortress was very tight and it was considered too risky. He would have to content himself with an aerial reconnaissance, though he did manage to get as close to the British frontier fence as he dared, disguised as a Spanish soldier.

On the isthmus, he noted the existence of heavily fortified machine gun bunkers constructed on the Spanish side of the frontier, but realised that the enemy guns from atop the Rock would quickly knock them out as soon as hostilities started.

Now he was in a better position to appreciate the difficulties of the operation ahead. The whole place was bristling with guns, aircraft and military vehicles and overflowing with soldiers. Although he had great admiration for the British preparations on the Fortress, he was confident that the German plan of attack could succeed.

This plan was for massive air raids using heavy Junker bombers from French Morocco, then by the more precise Stuka dive-bombers, hopefully from airfields within Spain. This, combined with the shelling from the batteries being constructed behind the Algeciras mountains and the bay, would force any ships in the harbour to leave. Just outside, in the Strait, the U-boats would be waiting. This would be followed by landings of special troops, on the northern seafront and behind the Rock, effected by small and fast landing craft. It was thought these would have a better chance of evading the guns. Finally a full armoured column would attack across the isthmus.

Even the use of the crack airborne troops who were so successful in the capture of the supposedly impregnable Ebba Emael fort in Belgium was considered in an earlier plan when the enigmatic Admiral Canaris was in charge of the operation. It had been hoped originally that these could be parachuted or landed with gliders on to the flats at the southern end of the Rock. Now the German high command had taken over direct control of the operation and they had learnt why it was that this proposed landing site was called the Windmill Hill Flats. The winds whipping round the end of the Rock or rising up the vertical cliffs from the sea could easily spell disaster for such a landing.

It was a plan that required meticulous preparation and precise synchronisation and special troops were already being trained in central France, in the Jura mountains, on similar rock formations as Gibraltar's, even to the extent of constructing tunnel systems within them. His task now was to evaluate the preparations achieved so far and the overall possibilities of the plan's success.

He toiled on relentlessly, trying to get everything organised, accumulating as much information as possible on the enemy. The whole area was crawling with secret agents both British and German as well as Spanish spies and counter spies. Some afternoons they would visit the grand Hotel Reina Cristina, a short way up from their villa on the seafront, for tea. There they would find groups of British Intelligence Officers sitting just a few tables away from them and he would wonder whether, in the same way as he recognised them, they also knew who the Germans were.

Then news finally arrived that the Führer was to meet with General Franco in Hendaye in the north of Spain. He had no doubt that soon after this official visit, orders for the operation to get underway would be given.

They waited apprehensively all that day, but it was not until late in the night that the news came. The meeting had been a fracas, there was no way that Hitler could accommodate the Caudillo's many conditions for his participation. Everything was postponed and he was to return to

Germany immediately. Through his bitter disappointment, the thought of that dreaded rail journey back through Spain made him quake.

The planning for the operation continued for a while after the Hendaye meeting, but once preparations for Barbarossa, the invasion of the Soviet Union, were initiated, they were abandoned and Gibraltar and the hinterland were spared the utter devastation that would surely have ensued had Operation Felix been carried out.

Shipwreck

24

1942 AD

In the aftermath of the storm, the battered merchantman sailed on, engines full ahead, trying desperately to regain the convoy from which it had become separated during the night. At this stage in the war, being alone in the Atlantic could be fatal, for German U-boats stealthily followed the large convoys and quickly dispatched any stragglers. As dawn broke the rising sun lit the eastern horizon, but no one saw the twin foaming tracks of the two racing torpedoes as they headed straight for the lonely ship. They struck the vessel midship and opened huge holes just below the water line.

For many of the crew this was their first ocean voyage, and so it was for young Jimmy. He had come off watch late that night and was still dozing in his bunk when the torpedoes struck. Realising immediately what had happened, he dashed on deck and with the help of the sailors already there managed to launch their lifeboat. They rowed desperately away from the now blazing and fast sinking ship and within five minutes she went down. Vainly they circled the area in the hope of finding any other survivors but there was no one, only a few scraps of flotsam to mark the spot where the vessel had disappeared. Seventeen of the crew were missing.

It was fortunate that the strong winds and heavy seas they had experienced since they had left Liverpool seemed to have spent themselves during the recent storm. With relatively calm seas, their worst enemy was the relentless sun and the fear of not being found before their water run out. They spent seven harrowing days in the boat until they were picked up by a Portuguese warship and it was on the island of Madeira, neutral in this war, that they were eventually landed. Some of the sailors were wounded and others were suffering from exposure, so they were all placed in a ward at the local hospital to recover.

One evening, after some of the fitter ones had ventured down into the town, two of Jim's friends came back excited. They had been over to the British school and had been invited by two of the girls to a tea party to be held there the following day.

That night one of these friends, no doubt still weak from the traumatic spell in the lifeboat, fell ill and begged Jim to go to the party in his place. Although he did not really feel up to this yet, Jim was finally persuaded to take his friend's place in the double date. It was a decision that was to change his life. Not only did he enjoy the party, but he also fell head over heels in love with the beautiful young girl, his partner for the evening by default.

After five weeks on this idyllic island, the shipwrecked crew was repatriated to England. A very distraught James vowed to see her again, even if he had to wait for the war to end. He was determined not to lose his new-found love. In this short time he had learnt all about her. She was from Gibraltar, the small British colony at the entrance to the Mediterranean, from where her family had been evacuated the previous year because of fears of a German invasion.

Fortunately the ship that was carrying them back home was diverted to Gibraltar at the last moment. The fortress was an austere place at this time; there were no women or children, just thousands of soldiers and sailors crammed into this very tiny peninsula. Once on the Rock he learnt that the Navy was recruiting strong swimmers to train as divers to counteract the night attacks by enemy frogmen on the shipping in the harbour. He promptly volunteered and in this way managed to stay on in Gibraltar.

Here he received instructions from the legendary Commander Crabb in the hazardous task of checking the hulls of ships for limpet mines and in patrolling the torpedo nets strung across the entrances to the harbour. Under these blue Mediterranean waters a fearful struggle went on, unseen and unheard by anyone, as the British divers fought the attacking enemy frogmen. It was only after the war that it became generally known that the enemy-manned torpedoes, crewed by Italian divers, were launched from a secret compartment cut into the bottom of an old tanker, the S.S. *Olterra,* anchored in the Spanish port of Algeciras across the bay.

In 1945 the evacuees from Madeira returned to the Rock and James was there awaiting his loved one. Within six weeks they were married. He stayed on in Gibraltar, raised his family there and became a respected member of the community and was amongst those leaders who fought for and eventually obtained many of the constitutional changes that made the old colony practically self-governing.

Homecoming

25

1944 AD

We were put to bed early for no one knew what the night held. I remember trying desperately to stay awake, wishing wholeheartedly for the sound of the siren. It would instantly transform an otherwise dull night into one of excitement and adventure. Sure enough, on most nights, especially in the early years, the deep mournful wail growing steadily to a long whine would fill the night and I would be up and shouting, 'La Sirena! La Sirena!' A sharp slap from my very frightened mother would soon put a stop to this as she struggled to get some warm clothing on us, left ready for just such an eventuality. I always tried to take a peek between the shiny blackout curtains at the dark world outside where the thin pencil beams of searchlights criss-crossed the skies. If I was lucky I would see them light up a barrage balloon floating like a great silver elephant in the night sky, or even an aeroplane, before I was unceremoniously yanked down to commence the long descent into the basement. The stairs would be full of other frightened mothers, some clutching their babies, hurrying on their sleepy children, the pace accelerating as distant booms heralded the approaching bombers.

Eventually we reached the dubious safety of the bare rooms in the labyrinthine basement of the large hotel. Most of the children would make for the far corner where a tall, grey-haired old lady sat. She would tell us the most thrilling and scary tales, no doubt to distract us from what was really happening. I heard my first version of Sweeney Todd from her and the finding of the finger in the meat pie featured in many of my nightmares for a long time thereafter.

If the crash of exploding bombs came nearer, our mothers would rush to get us and hold the family close together. A deathly hush would fall on the place interrupted only by terrible explosions, whimpers of fear and the soft drone of muttered prayers.

There must have been some opening from the basement to the street for the few men there were would gather by this and glean information of how the raid was going, probably from passing air-raid wardens, and keep us informed. One night the stark announcement that 'Las Carmelitas' had been hit was followed by great lamentation, for this was the parish church of many Gibraltarian families who lived in the hotels around it across the park. Once the 'All Clear' finally sounded and we climbed wearily back to our rooms, the view from the windows on a clear night could be spectacular as the burning buildings turned the black night crimson.

When incendiary bombs were used, we would sometimes meet the men coming down from the roof with fire buckets laden with the small narrow bombs which they had doused. We boys would eye each other in anticipation, for this meant that the usual search for shrapnel the following morning would be enhanced by the chance of finding one of these spent bombs.

The park across the road would be pock-marked with circles of white ash where the incendiaries had fallen and we would be over there early, searching and making the lives of the poor park keepers, mostly old men or war veterans, a misery. They had probably hoped for a quiet time as most of the English children had been removed to safer places away from London and the air raids.

My prize possession and the envy of all my friends was one of these incendiary bombs. Its front half melted on the ground and its long flukes standing up on end made a magnificent trophy. Unfortunately my mother refused even to contemplate my bringing it back to Gibraltar. She wanted nothing that would remind her of these terrible times.

In later years there were those excruciating tense moments when the faint droning motors of a V-1 suddenly stopped somewhere above us and everyone fearfully held their breath until the booming explosion released the tension.

It was the advent of these dreaded flying bombs that convinced many mothers that we would be safer in the Underground stations, so every evening we would cross the streets and, carrying our bedding with us, spend the night there. It was fascinating, the trains rumbling in full of soldiers and sailors, the young Gibraltarian couples strolling up and down the platform in a macabre echo of the Main Street 'paseo' of yesteryear. Again I remember trying to stay awake for as long as possible for the story amongst the boys was that the very last train of the night was a jet black one – I never saw it.

This adventure unfortunately came to an abrupt end, for one morning, as we were all returning to the hotel, the siren sounded. It is the one time when I can recall the sheer panic of our mothers being transmitted to us children. We ran frightened through the empty streets with our bedding streaming behind us, urged on desperately by terrorised mothers. We never went to the Underground again.

It was shortly after this that early one morning there was a knock on our door. My mother opened and a tall man with a long list of names just said, 'You're on it'. I have never forgotten my poor mother crying and jumping around the room. We were being repatriated. We were going home. And so it was that I missed the biggest bangs of all – the V-2s, but then I gather they were not all that exciting. Just a big boom which, if particularly loud, was liable to be the last thing you ever heard.

Much later I realised that for our nerve-racked mothers it must have all been a very harrowing experience as they struggled to control their children single-handed in an alien and very dangerous environment. These women were not the independent, much-travelled, and completely bilingual mothers of today. They were housewives in the literal sense of the word. Most had hardly ever left Gibraltar and many spoke little English before they were wrenched, the majority husbandless, from house and home and with their children, some mere babes in arms, thrust into the cauldron of war. Daily they scoured the almost bare London food shops in the hope of finding anything that would augment the sparse rations for their children.

Soon we were being taken northwards, first to a camp just across the border in Scotland. Here we city children, whose only experience of the countryside were the London parks, had a wonderful time. I remember on that first evening at the camp coming across a semi-circle of boys all standing in awe staring at the centre where squatted a large fat toad. None of us would dare stand directly in front of it for fear of the toad's renowned ability to spit poison. It was not until the following morning when we found the toad in exactly the same spot that we realised that it was dead and had probably been dead for a long time. This innocence was not to last long and in the three weeks that we spent at the camp all the small ponds and streams in the vicinity were denuded of frogs, tadpoles, toads, newts and anything else that moved.

Eventually we were bussed down to the coast, to the port of Glasgow. Here we were herded into vast empty warehouses. Long queues of wide-eyed pale mothers trying desperately to hold on to their excited and unruly children, all clad in the drab colours of the war years, greatcoats mostly black, grey or brown, with the tell-tale tags bearing name and group tied to their lapels. At last we emerged into what seemed to be a high-sided corridor. One side though, we soon realised, was actually the grey flank of a huge liner into which the front of the long lines of weary evacuees were already laboriously climbing.

The following morning we found that the ship had moved during the night and we were anchored in the middle of a wide river. Here we waited impatiently for some days until one day we woke to find everything reverberating and guessed that we were on our way at last. We rushed on deck only to find that all was grey yet again. Grey foggy skies and slate-grey seas. This went on for days, the constant throbbing and the grey vistas. The only thrill was when someone briefly spotted a sleek destroyer, one of our escorts, speeding through the swirling mists. Then one morning, as we climbed up to the deck, a shaft of yellow light welcomed us. What a glorious sight awaited us. The sun was shining and the sky was blue, a blue that few of us could remember, even the sea was a lovely deep blue. On the horizon we could just make out the line of low hills of a distant coastline. The air was electric with excitement, but we boys blissfully played on, now in our vests in the hot sunshine, an unheard-of luxury. As the ship sailed onwards, the rolling hills gave way to mountain ranges and before long another lofty range was visible on the other side of the ship, both getting closer as the passage narrowed.

Suddenly we found that the playing deck had mysteriously emptied. We were alone, but only until our frantic mothers came and hurried us away to the front of the ship. Everyone seemed to be there. Transfixed, staring forwards in anticipation as the ship sped ahead. Now and again there were excited shouts and even snatches of song and then, as if by magic, a total silence as in the distance what looked like a small island appeared to detach itself from the inexorable mountainous coast. It was at that moment that I heard a single sob and looking back, beheld one of the few men that had come with us. He towered above me – all men look tall when you are a small boy. I gazed in wonder as the tears coursed down his cheeks. I had never realised that men also cried.

Chaos soon broke out on the deck and amidst the crying and kissing I looked out at the distant island rapidly getting bigger, a whitish-green rock dazzling in the afternoon sun and realised that this was it, this was the Rock of Gibraltar. This was our homeland.

We had left behind many who would still have to endure more bombings and even another evacuation to Northern Ireland. For these it was to be the third such evacuation. We had all been shipped to French Morocco at the start of the war, but had to be taken out hurriedly and precariously three weeks later when France capitulated, only to be evacuated again within a few weeks to England, Madeira and even as far away as Jamaica. Most of the refugees were repatriated by 1947, but another four long years were to elapse before the last of them were brought back. This anguish and suffering helped meld this now almost three hundred year old community into a people with an identity all their own, the Gibraltarians.

The Last Siege

26

1965 AD

Antonio had worked in the dockyard in Gibraltar for thirty years. Every working day of his life for as long as he could remember he had travelled back and forth from his home in the frontier town of La Linea. He was tired of doing so, but grateful for the work. There was no way he could make half as much money working in his own country, that is if he could find a job at all. True, the Spanish authorities made him exchange his hard-earned sterling into pesetas at very low rates when he crossed back, but even then it was well worth it, especially as he was able to exchange all his overtime wages in Gibraltar at a much higher rate. He could also augment this with the purchase of commodities not available at home. In this way he provided well for his wife and the apple of his eye, his only daughter Mari. He doted on her, but she was growing up fast and he was starting to worry for her future.

Sometimes there would be lengthy delays in crossing the frontier, with long queues and unpleasant body searches and he resented this, but realised that his country's authorities had to maintain some control at the frontier to prevent the English doing what they liked. El Caudillo, that is General Franco, was right, these usurpers of their land had to be put in their place and Gibraltar restored to the nation. Lately things had been getting worse and the officials at the frontier stricter. He had even lost some trinkets he had been bringing over for Mari.

It was May when Mari met Johnny. She was just sixteen and it had happened before his very own eyes, at the dance held annually in honour of the Virgin in the patio where they lived. She had danced with this Llanito, a Gibraltarian, under the watchful eyes of his wife and all their neighbours, and that had been it. They had fallen in love and no amount of pleading on his part would dissuade her. His wife though was all for the young couple, for she realised that her daughter's future would be assured and prosperous. He knew that she was right, but found it hard to stomach her marrying a foreigner, least of all a British one from the Rock. In any event it would mean grandchildren, the one thing he had been looking forward to for a long time.

So they were married and Mari went to live in Gibraltar. He would see her every day on his way back from work, but it wasn't the same. Time passed and there were no babies, he was getting old and apprehensive. Meanwhile, at the frontier the situation was worsening. Already the Spanish authorities had stopped the issue of new passes and now it appeared that all the women workers were to lose their passes. Nevertheless he was sure that nothing would happen to him. Spain was still recovering from the devastations of the Civil War and her isolation after the Second World War and desperately needed the sterling she got from the thousands of dockyard workers. The audacity of the English in having their queen visit the Rock had started all these troubles and things had been deteriorating ever since. Whilst he ranted and raved against them at home he could not say a word about it at his daughter's for she would not allow any discussion of politics there.

It was in the middle of all these tribulations that his daughter announced that she was pregnant. He was overjoyed. The baby was due in August. How he longed for and counted the days for this happy event when at last he could hold his grandchild in his arms! He hoped it would be a girl, for then he would be able to relive those happy memories when he was younger and Mari had been his very own baby.

Then the unbelievable happened. The frontier was to be closed. What was worse, all communications were to be terminated with the colony, the Algeciras ferry was to be stopped, the telephone lines were to be cut off and even the mail was to be re-routed via Madrid and England. Up to the very last moment he refused to believe it and thought that it was all a bluff to force the English to offer some concessions on their sovereignty over the Rock. With growing anxiety and sorrow he watched his daughter getting bigger. Hastily they made tentative arrangements to try to communicate on a fixed day every week by shouting across the hundred-metre strip of no man's land that separated the two frontier fences. Even if the worst came to the worst and they did close the gates, he just could not believe that it would be for very long.

But the frontier was closed and for all of sixteen years. Not only was he separated from his beloved daughter and his grandchild-to-be, but he also lost his job without the prospect of finding another. Around him his younger neighbours started to migrate to northern European countries where they could find work and send money back home to their families. Ironically, many went to England. He was too old now for this and in any case it would be unthinkable to leave his wife and go even further from his Mari.

It was not until a week after the birth that Antonio learnt that he had a baby granddaughter. Two more weeks elapsed before he caught his first glimpse of her across the two frontier fences. That godforsaken strip of land was to become his rendezvous every Wednesday at noon, rain or shine. Soon he learnt to pray for a Wednesday without rain or without what could be worse, a strong Levanter. For then this persistent easterly wind would make communications impossible and even the strongest shout would not carry across that wasteland. From his meagre savings he managed to scrape together enough money to buy himself a second-hand pair of binoculars. With these, as the years went by, he was able to watch as his beloved granddaughter, held aloft by Mari, grew up. How he longed to hold her and hug her, but despite his wife's entreaties, he stubbornly refused to cross the Strait and go to the Rock via Algeciras and Morocco. Antonio still clung to the hope that the frontier would reopen. His granddaughter was seven years old and had just gone through a bout of measles when his wife finally convinced him to make the crossing. He wasn't getting any younger and there was no real sign that the frontier would be opened.

On a blustery September day, he boarded the ferry at Algeciras, crossed to Africa and then on another ferry set sail from Tangier back across the Strait to Gibraltar. That evening, as the vessel neared the Rock and after a whole day spent travelling, he gazed again at Algeciras just across the Bay, the port from which he had set sail early that morning and mused bitterly on the inhumanity of politics. Despite the by then strong winds, he persisted in staying out on deck getting ever more excited as the Rock loomed bigger and bigger. It was there, right at the very front of the ship, that his distraught wife finally found him sitting on one of the benches staring out at the great Rock as the ship came alongside. On the quay she could just make out her daughter holding little Toni by the hand, both waving desperately. As she glanced sideways at her husband to see whether he had spotted them, she realised with dismay and panic that the staring eyes were fixed and unseeing.

Indeed they were never to see again. Two days later, in what was widely reported in Spain as a magnanimous gesture by the Franco regime, the frontier gates were opened just long enough to allow the remains of Antonio Jesús Martín back into his hometown for burial.

Operación Calpe

27

2015 AD

It was a damp, cold and moonless night in early November. Across the isthmus, banks of sea mist rolled in from the Mediterranean, at times enveloping everything in their path in a grey impenetrable shroud. At three o'clock precisely, two vehicles drew up by each police post on either side of the runway and the Services Police on duty there were taken into custody. Two other men also dressed as Services Police replaced them. At exactly the same time, groups of civilians coming from Spain and out from Gibraltar seized control of the frontier post. Policemen, frontier guards and revenue officers were all taken quietly and driven away. It was all done swiftly and efficiently and took everyone entirely by surprise. No one had noticed the soldiers coming in throughout the day disguised as tourists. Then more soldiers crossing from the eastern side of the frontier fence captured the RAF guard patrol at that end of the runway. It was now the turn of the control tower and the ancillary services that were manned at night. Fortunately, two of the Spanish officers with the invading team had been amongst the NATO officers who had been given a tour of the tower and airport facilities earlier in the year. Everything went according to plan and, barring a few minor hitches, all the key sites were captured without the alarm being raised. The services quarters in the area were all surrounded, but not interfered with. The airport terminal was empty; no planes were expected on this night.

As soon as this was accomplished, large numbers of troops that had been hidden in strategic places in the hinterland were transported into Gibraltar. They immediately crossed the runway and commenced erecting a huge barbed wire fence along its edge, stretching from Eastern Beach to the tip on the west side. The only access through this was at the road crossing and here a series of barriers across the road were erected to control the passage. This section was not put in place until the very last moment. Up to this point, all pedestrian and vehicular traffic coming through here and from Spain was redirected to a holding area after being divested of any mobile phones and other means of communications. It had all taken under two hours. The only casualty in the operation had been one of the RAF guard dogs at the eastern end of the runway, which had to be silenced when it would not stop barking. The officer concerned was later severely reprimanded – the Spaniards were apprehensive about British sensitivity regarding animals.

In Gibraltar no one knew about any of this for the first hour. The police patrol car doing its rounds at 4 am was taken into custody. Police headquarters attempted to establish radio contact with this car without success, but it was only after there had been a few calls by the families of those on duty at the frontier that night, enquiring whether there was anything wrong with the phones there, that any suspicions were aroused. All the telephones in the area had of course been disconnected. When at 4.30 another patrol car was sent down to investigate and failed to report in, the police attempted to contact the tower and various other offices at the airport. All of these failed to respond and the alarm was raised. A couple of police cars approached the area cautiously only to be confronted with the Spanish soldiers busy erecting the barriers at the runway crossing.

Calls were immediately made to the governor, Fortress Headquarters and the chief minister. It was too late, when the few British troops stationed in Gibraltar aided by those of the Gibraltar Regiment available at this early hour arrived: the fence was in place and guarded by hundreds of Spanish soldiers. Spain, in a superbly co-ordinated military operation, had effectively severed the isthmus and taken control of the airport. All of those in custody were then released and those cars in the holding area allowed to continue their journey.

The Foreign Office in London was informed, the Spanish ambassador summoned, and the urgent necessity of dispatching reinforcements taken up with the War Office. Of course there was now no possibility of sending these out by air. Warships would have to be prepared to sail immediately. Later that day there was uproar in both the Houses of Parliament, with the government assuring everyone that they were monitoring the situation closely.

The news spread like wildfire through the town. Gibraltar was stunned and the people took to the streets. Very soon a large and very angry crowd made up of most of the adult population, set off for the airport with the intention of storming through. Well before reaching the newly erected Spanish fence, the British and Gibraltar Regiment troops stopped them. There, urged on by their sense of utter impotence, the frustrated crowds hurled abuse at Spain and Europe and anyone else they could think of. There were even those who suspected collusion by the British government in this dastardly act. Certainly they felt betrayed at having been left so defenceless and were suspicious at the ease with which the Spaniards had captured the airport.

At the European Commission headquarters in Brussels, hasty meetings were called. It was unthinkable that two fellow members of the Union should confront each other in this way over such a small place. A team of high-ranking officials was immediately dispatched to the area and the Spanish representatives called in to explain their country's actions. It was not till late in the afternoon that Spain issued its statement.

> 'The occupation of the airport is only temporary and has been undertaken in the interest and well-being of all the inhabitants of the area. The intransigence of the residents of the British colony at Gibraltar has prevented the implementation of the Airport Agreement of 1987. This Agreement, which everyone knew would greatly enhance the economic viability of the whole region, had been agreed to by the United Kingdom and endorsed by the European Union. Once the provisions of this agreement are put in place and functioning, Spain will revert to the previous position and the troops will be recalled.
>
> This in no way affects Spain's traditional and irrevocable claim to the isthmus occupied unilaterally by Britain in the 1930s. It is hoped that the direct benefits accrued to the inhabitants on both sides of the frontier will help convince the residents of Gibraltar of the wisdom of this operation. In the meantime the airport will carry on functioning as normal.'

In the end, a deal was brokered at Brussels between Spain and Britain. The frontier would be reinstated as hitherto at Four Corners and the Airport Agreement implemented. EU funds would be made available for the construction of a tunnel under the airstrip and the addition of another runway, if this was found to be feasible. Further funds would also be allotted for infrastructure and improvements. These included the construction of two new terminals, the one on the Spanish side of the frontier to be provided with direct underground access to the airport. The Spaniards also undertook to ease restrictions at the frontier by reintroducing the double traffic lanes both in and out and the institution of red and green channels.

There was much anger, bitterness and a deep sense of betrayal in Gibraltar, but what was entirely unexpected was the uproar in the Spanish Cortés as the opposition parties vented their fury at what they claimed was a Spanish retreat from recovered national territory. The whole operation appeared to have backfired on the prime minister. For many years, the Gibraltar problem had been used by the ruling parties in Spain whenever it became necessary to divert public opinion from unpleasant domestic policies or when things were not going favourably. Perhaps it is just as well that no one in Gibraltar ever heard the words of the Spanish premier to the leader of the opposition when, in an attempt to calm things down, he had a private session with him. 'You know that we have always had the ability of strangling the British colony at Gibraltar by using that frontier post. Today, with this agreement, we have placed our finger on its jugular.'

The Miracle

28

2062 AD

Finally, after so many years, the Roman Catholic church in Gibraltar obtained the go-ahead to build a shrine near the top of the Rock. There were to be many restrictions. It would be quite a small chapel and only subdued lighting would be allowed. There would be no vehicular access. Nevertheless the church authorities were happy that they would be able to achieve their long-cherished ambition. There were even plans to erect the Stations of the Cross leading up to the shrine at a later stage. Many of the towns in neighbouring Spain have such Calvaries on nearby hills or mountains.

After much deliberation, a suitable site was selected on the road running along the crest of the Rock. There was a sharp indentation leading to a rock shelter in what appeared to have been a small cave, the front part of which had apparently fallen in at some time in the past. The relatively flat surface thus formed made an ideal floor for the little chapel. From the site there was a splendid view of the bay and from the top you could even see the sandy beaches on the eastern coast of Spain winding their way northwards right up to where the river Guadiaro flows out into the sea. The architect in charge proposed to build this shrine facing out towards the west using the rugged limestone rock wall of the shelter as background to the altar.

Work started with much help from volunteers from the various religious societies. Getting the materials up there and bringing down the debris was an arduous and slow process but the works continued steadily.

Finally the little chapel was complete and the date for its inauguration was set for the 20th August, this being the feast of St Bernard, the patron saint of Gibraltar, and the anniversary of the final recapture of the Rock from the Moors by the Christian forces of Spain six hundred years ago.

The night before the ceremony the volunteers gave the whole place a thorough cleaning. They even polished the age-old encrusted rocks behind and above the altar. The next day, a long procession led by representative groups of children from all the schools who had been bussed up to the St Michael's Cave level made its way slowly up the Rock. There was obviously not much room in the chapel and most of the congregation just stood along the road where the ceremony was relayed to them on giant television screens placed at intervals on the hill. Inside the floodlit shrine, numerous television cameras recorded the event for them and those viewing at home.

It was as the inaugural Mass reached its holiest moment, the Consecration, when the bishop held up the chalice, that it happened. All eyes were raised towards the little altar and the chalice gleaming in the bright flood of light when one of the youngest children in the front pew uttered the one word, 'Fish'. All eyes were immediately riveted on the rough rock wall above the golden chalice. There was no mistaking it: there on a flat piece of the limestone was the indisputable shape of a fish. All the cameras immediately zoomed in on this apparition and so the phenomenon was viewed by all those on the hill and everyone watching at home.

Remarkably, the bishop kept his cool and in the midst of his now stunned flock finished the mass. Once the ceremony was over, everyone wanted to come in and see the wondrous manifestation. There could be no doubt about it. On the small section of flat rock, high above the ground, the perfect silhouette of a fish had been etched. It had obviously been done many years ago as the outline was very faint and was only visible when the floodlights were turned on. When and how no one could tell. Someone mentioned that this had been the sign of the early Christians and it was not long before many were claiming it as a miracle.

It was to be quite a while before experts came to examine the relatively simple etching and in the meantime, the many people who flocked to the shrine daily started claiming miraculous healings and favours granted to those who prayed there. In the end and after many tests were carried out on the rock and the actual etching, these experts reported it as having been carved approximately two thousand years ago and therefore dating back to the middle Roman period. They confirmed that this type of fish symbol, the Ichthus, had been the universal sign of the Christians and was frequently used by them throughout the Empire at this time. The letters of the Greek word for fish made up the initials for 'Jesus Christ, Son of God, Saviour' in that language.

We will probably never know who or why this fish symbol came to be carved in this cave on top of the Rock. Could it have been used as a shelter by early Christians, maybe fleeing from Roman persecutions? It was the floodlighting of the cave that had revealed the etching which no doubt had been exposed the previous night by all the scrubbing and polishing of the rocks. Perhaps the real miracle is the fact that, without knowing of its existence, this particular spot was the one selected for the building of the holy shrine.

The Promised Land

29

2095 AD

Over the past hundred years the differences between the developed countries and the third world had continued to increase inexorably. The utter devastation brought about in Africa by the dreaded Aids epidemic and other new infectious diseases had decimated the population and halted much of the progress on this continent. This contrasted sharply with the spectacular success of the European Federation. People from all over Africa, desperate to get away from the poverty, disease and malnutrition, kept trekking north to the Mediterranean littoral in a determined effort to try and get into Europe. For generations the annual return home during their summer vacations of those Africans lucky enough to work in Europe, loaded with consumer goods and obviously quite prosperous, only served to highlight the enormous disparity in living standards and this attracted new waves of immigrants.

Across the Strait, the population in Morocco had increased dramatically as more and more people from further south arrived there and conditions were said to be appalling. Every month, for years now, many were drowned at night whilst attempting to cross the narrow stretch of water that separates the two continents. Many more were intercepted and returned by the European patrol system operating from Gibraltar, Algeciras and Tarifa. Who knows how many were successful and managed to get through. Even then, the strict requirements of identity papers and work permits in the Federation meant that some of these were eventually caught and repatriated.

This precarious situation reached a climax in sixty-two and the numbers trying to get across the Strait only diminished when an epidemic broke out and quickly spread through the squalid collection of camps scattered along the coast and wiped out thousands. Soon though the pressure was on again. Governments on the North African coast tottered as dissension gained ground because of the dreadful conditions.

Eventually, based on the success of the Green March on the Spanish Sahara when, over a hundred years earlier, thousands of Moroccans had marched into the Spanish colony and overwhelmed the authorities there, the idea of trying a similar thing, only this time over the sea across the Strait, spread through the camps. They were desperate and starving. In this way maybe they would be able to swamp the patrol vessels with sheer numbers. Efforts by the European Federation to get the Moroccan government to stop this failed, as that government was now almost powerless.

Thousands of boats were massed on the southern side of the Strait, many hastily constructed and consisting of a few boards nailed together and completely unseaworthy. On the night of the first day of July 2073 they had all set off for Europe, the Promised Land. A flotilla of Federation warships tried to prevent them getting through, but many made it. Countless numbers were drowned in the melée. For weeks after this reckless exodus, dead bodies were still being washed up on the beaches on both sides of the Strait. On land, the armed forces rounded up most of those who had been lucky enough to make it and huge camps were set up. When it was all over, attempts to repatriate these unfortunate people were frustrated because Morocco would not take them back, justifiably claiming that most were not Moroccan anyway. The result was chaos and conditions in these temporary camps soon deteriorated as negotiations became protracted.

An international conference held in Gibraltar to try to resolve the problem proved fruitless. In the end some of the immigrants, the really lucky ones, were allowed to stay on under a quota system and moved northwards. In fact Europe, with its ageing populations caused by an ever-decreasing birth rate, needed them. Not only did they undertake all those unskilled jobs essential to any community which were no longer attractive to the affluent Europeans, but their tax contributions helped support this ageing society. The rest, in one of those shameful acts of history, were forcibly landed on the African coast by European vessels. The Second Gibraltar Conference, held two years after these tragic events, set new and improved immigrant quotas for the different regions of the European

Federation and established an enhanced system of grant aid for the poorer African countries. It was hoped that this, together with the mass production of the latest vaccines to control the new infectious diseases, would improve the standards of living there and thus stop the flood of people northwards.

I have a greater interest in all of this than most, for it was a few days after the mass sailing that my father, whilst fishing off Europa Point, found the half-drowned girl. He told me the story many times of how on that day, just before sunset he came across a large log floating in the sea with what, he assumed at the time, to be a dead body lying across it. Yet another of those poor drowned Africans, he assumed. Examining it closer though he thought he saw some signs of life and, rowing right up to the log, he managed to haul the limp and soaking body into his boat and was startled to find that it was actually a young woman and a beautiful one at that. With difficulty he was able to revive her.

On the way back to port he speculated on what he should do. If he notified the police, as he should, she would be promptly sent back to the chaos across the Strait, that is, if she survived the camps on this side. The more he looked at her the more he knew he could never do this. In the end, under the cover of darkness, he brought her home. He lived alone with his mother in a big house surrounded by gardens at the southern end of the Rock. It was thanks to his mother's kind heart and ingenuity that they managed over the years to keep Aysha, for that was her name, from being discovered. In the end she was accepted by those few who saw her as a live-in maid. I used to love hearing my father tell this story. Unfortunately, Aysha died whilst I was still a baby, so I never got to know her.

I now live alone with my elderly grandmother; my father died last year, a grumpy bachelor. It was my granny who finally told me that I was not actually adopted.

Utopia

30

2133 AD

To go up to the top of the Rock and look eastwards to view the creation of the new land was one of the wonders in those days. The two horn-like projections extended further into the Mediterranean with each visit, until eventually they encompassed what were to become the new Catalan Bay and Sandy Bay coves of today. I can recall my grandfather telling me fascinating stories his father had told him about the thrill, when, as a young boy, he had seen the reclamation of a large part of the harbour almost one hundred and fifty years ago. He said the old man would stop suddenly in the middle of the street when they were going to the supermarket or the hospital and say nostalgically, 'Right here, where we are standing now, I once caught a lovely ten-pound bass,' or, 'There, by that bus stop, we would come to collect the best bait prawns'. He would also tell him tales of mysterious explosions on the new land, caused by discarded landmines ditched in the sea at the end of the last world war. These kept turning up in the sand used for the reclamation, which was dredged from the depth of the Strait. There were no mines this time, but the large reclamations carried out on the East Side were surely much more spectacular.

This exciting project, which had started in a small way as far back as the end of the 1990s, was finally finished ten years ago and the new land formed is now the famous Gibraltar Lido. Dedicated totally to tourism and leisure, the Lido's superb beaches put an end to the Rock's shortage of good beaches and these are now lined with tall hotels, yacht marinas and the new casino. The coves themselves provide ideal shelter from both the prevailing east and west winds, but what is best of all, the whole area is away from that bugbear of Gibraltar town, the Levanter cloud. In fact the moderate east winds so common here are ideal on the Lido, whilst the

Rock itself shields it from the westerlies. All of this has contributed greatly in placing the Rock amongst the most popular of the Mediterranean resorts, especially with British tourists.

Two of the measures taken towards the end of the troubles with Spain, before the establishment of the European Federation, have also gone a long way towards making Gibraltar so successful. There was a policy of encouraging retired people from the United Kingdom to settle here and thus strengthen the ties with Britain when these were becoming tenuous. Eventually these expatriates, attracted by the warm and sunny weather, English legal system and low taxes, formed a substantial proportion of the population. This not only attracted their families and friends to visit here, but also made the place seem even more British, which in turn made it more appealing to tourists from Britain. The other, of course, was the enlargement of the airport together with the addition of the extra runway and tunnels all accomplished with European funds, fruits of the traumatic problems with Spain all those years ago. Nowadays Gibraltar has direct air links with many European cities and even across the Atlantic.

There is now a truly spectacular and unique attraction. One that no other resort can come close to imitating. It has even topped the famous Rock Apes in popularity. No visitor to Gibraltar today can leave without doing the new Tunnel Tour. These tunnels were first opened to the public over a hundred years ago and the tour has continued to be extended and improved ever since. Now you are bussed deep into the centre of the Rock through well-lit wide roads, past vintage army hospitals, barracks, and kitchens cut into the solid limestone and dating back to the terrible world wars of the final century of the last millennium. You visit vast water tanks carved out of the very heart of the Rock and huge natural caves festooned with stalagmites and stalactites surrounding pools of crystal-clear water. There are even theatres for films and concerts. Then down to the base of the mountain to view the old military storerooms, deep down where no enemy fire could ever reach them, full of giant shells, mighty guns and even tanks. Continuing right through the Rock, at times coming out onto great balconies with stunning views, made all the more spectacular because you are never quite sure where it is that you are going to emerge. Some of these journeys are on escalators, others on moving platforms. The finale, when elevators shoot you up to the very top of the Rock on to a revolving restaurant with those magnificent views spanning two continents, is a gloriously fitting end.

One very interesting find was made in a small section of St Michael's Cave during the excavations and tunnel connections when this tour was being constructed. This had been sealed by an internal rock fall many years ago and never accessed until now. In it were found a Roman shield and a couple of swords and other items which seemed to indicate that a small contingent of Roman soldiers was stationed there. Roman remains are comparatively rare on the Rock and it has always been thought that their presence on the Rock was minimal. However this find would appear to indicate that they did keep troops here. Or could it be that they were soldiers on the run using the cave to hide in?

Only the tunnel systems at the very southern tip of the Rock are out of bounds. Here the military is still very much in occupation, for across the Strait looms Africa and its now developing countries and their burgeoning populations. There are rumours of missile silos, nuclear arsenals and submarine pens with secret underwater access and sophisticated radar installations for monitoring vessels passing in and out of the Strait.

Gibraltar, that great fortress of yesteryear, has been miraculously transformed into an ideal tourist resort, albeit one which may be sitting on a virtual time bomb.

The Reef

31

2157 AD

It was in this year that the new venture, after much opposition, was finally started at Rosia Bay. The initial idea of closing the bay and using it for fattening tuna caught in the Strait for the Japanese market, had long since been abandoned because of the scarcity of these fish. The Dolphinarium, which had previously been sited here, had been moved to the new Lido. Now this historic bay, which had sheltered the *Victory* with Nelson's body on board after the battle of Trafalgar, was to be enclosed and used as a fish farm to produce that exquisite but alas now rare sea bass. This fish, known locally as the *robalo* and in Spain as the *lubina,* had been called the ranger by generations of British soldiers stationed on the Rock during the days of Empire. No doubt this was because of its habit of patrolling inshore waters where it was one of the top predators. To the French it is the *loup de mer*, the sea wolf. It was said that no stroll along the sea walls or moles in spring or summer was complete without catching a glimpse of these magnificent fish, often making lightning attacks on the profuse numbers of bogues, mackerel and many other bait shoals that were so common then. Most of these had now practically disappeared and without their prey, the bass also vanished.

This dearth of fish now made fish farming highly profitable, especially for this much sought-after fish that could always be relied upon to fetch a good price. For years now, heavy over-fishing of the seas, particularly within the Mediterranean, had devastated fish stocks. In fact the Strait, because of its strategic position between two large bodies of water, was one of the few places where fish of any size were still being caught. So far the very controversial policy of seeding the seas with millions of cloned fry did not seem to be having a marked effect.

Here it had been decided to go for the real thing, and the farm was started by using the roe from the now rare catches of bass made in the Strait, usually by the few remaining expert fishermen from Catalan Bay, the only ones who were still catching them. Eventually of course, when the farmed fish matured, their roe was used. Within five years the farm was making a substantial profit, set to increase as the price of fresh fish continued to soar. It was after all an ideal place for such a venture: well protected against storms and with substantial quantities of fresh seawater surging in and out daily. Although not comparable with other areas where huge bays, inlets and fjords were being enclosed to breed fish, it was large enough to cater for local demand as well as for the booming tourist trade on the far side of the Rock.

Gilthead, the *doradas*, were also kept. These were relatively easy to rear, as brackish lagoons along the coast had always been one of their favourite haunts. Unfortunately attempts at keeping that most famous of Mediterranean fish, the delicious red mullet, the *salmonete*, had not been successful. This would have provided a great bonanza, this fish fetching top price as it has done since the days of Rome over two thousand years ago. In fact the Romans had had to introduce legislation to control their exorbitant market price.

Just offshore along this rocky coast an artificial reef had been created by the conservationists many years ago. In recent years a tunnel had been constructed on the seabed leading from the shore at Camp Bay to two underwater viewing platforms. One wonders what the view of this reef would have been like in days gone by when it is said that this bay was renowned for its moray eels, octopus and many other species, including the giant groupers, which then lived quite close inshore. Despite the shortage of fish now, the view was still spectacular and very popular with tourists, particularly when a rare shoal of squid arrived before total darkness set in. More intriguing was the occasional sighting of small shoals of very colourful fish usually associated with tropical waters; a sure sign of the slow but inexorable warming of the planet

The flora and fauna on land were also under threat as more and more people from the north of the Federation came to live in the south seeking the sun and warmth. A drive to Malaga up the famed Costa del Sol now offered barely a glimpse of the shoreline and in fact the sea was only really seen when the road climbed above the tall structures lining the whole of the coast. This plethora of buildings had spread inland and the popularity of rural tourism had also had an effect up in the mountains. Nor had the steadily increasing dryness of the weather helped, as even the smallest rivers were dammed in order to conserve as much water as possible, flooding many beautiful valleys. This was happening to a lesser extent throughout Europe as the affluent society spread out into the countryside. The impact on wildlife was devastating, as wide areas of their habitat vanished. The spectacular passage of thousands of raptors, storks and all manner of birds for which the Rock had been famous as they migrated in early autumn and spring from most of western Europe across the Strait and back was greatly diminished. Desperate efforts to try to stem this tide resulted in large numbers joining conservation societies and ecologists everywhere had become very influential.

At first it seemed as if the fish farm was beneficial to the reef, as fish appeared to increase in numbers, no doubt attracted by the spillage of food emanating from there. However within a couple of years, as had been predicted, it was noticed that much of the sea life on the reef near the front of Rosia Bay was dying and the battle was on. There were to be many confrontations and demonstrations over the fish farm. The frantic owners tried all manner of things, filters, new feeds, nets, but to no avail. The detritus emanating from the thousands of fish within the enclosure could not be contained, as the constant passage of fresh seawater was essential for their survival. Eventually, after seven years of operation, the fish farm was shut down and the wonderful artificial reef was rescued – for a while longer at least.

The White Narcissus

32

2200 AD

Extract from
Minutes of the Gibraltar Archaeological Society
1st June, 2200

The President opened the proceedings by mentioning his regret at the poor attendance and attributed this to the lack of interest from which the Society has suffered for the last ten years. Gibraltar is a small place and its fascinating history and long prehistory has now practically all been thoroughly studied. Its many richly-endowed caves have all been dug up. It was unfortunate that despite the substantial and valuable material uncovered over the years they had not found the ultimate prize, that is another Neanderthal skull. All must agree though that what had been discovered has gone a long way in establishing the compelling prehistory of this Rock of ours and indeed contributed substantially to the prehistory of the rest of Europe. In any case, of the three small skull fragments found recently, two have been identified as belonging to the Neanderthal period.

Regarding the small statue found at Gorham's Cave at the end of the final dig there, it has now been confirmed that this is of Phoenician origin dated 1000 BC to 800 BC. It probably represents Astarte or Asherah, the Lady of the Sea, both of which were worshipped by the Phoenicians as goddesses associated with the sea at different periods. It matched the smaller statuettes and other items found in this cave at the start of the excavations here many years ago in what is thought to have become a shrine to Herakles. The small lamps, scarabs, rings and other objects found scattered around would seem to indicate that these were votive offerings to the gods left here in gratitude, presumably by sailors as the cave is not readily accessible from above.

Finally, it was with great enthusiasm that the President announced the recent discovery of two new caves at the far end of the Rock. One of these is not much more than a rock shelter but the other, though small, is deep, dry and shows much promise. Both these caves had been uncovered during the works in connection with the building of one of the balconies for the new southern extension to the ever-popular Rock Tunnel Tour. These works had entailed the removal of some shale slopes and in the process a rock ledge had been uncovered on to which both these caves opened.

He had contacted the Oxford University Group and the Natural History Museum in England, both of whom had undertaken so much of the work on the caves here previously. They had already liaised with their European counterparts and are now in the process of selecting a team to come out and, with our collaboration and that of the local museum staff, carry out both digs using the most thorough and up-to-date methods available. He promised to keep members informed of the progress of these arrangements and hoped that the discovery of these new caves would help in revitalising the Society.

The team that would carry out the excavations was finally assembled two months later. Initial ultra-sound and radar depth scanning of the cave floors had indicated the presence of layers of organic material including bone fragments, so the dig started amidst great expectations. However the excavation of the larger cave floor proved singularly barren. Anyone could follow the works in progress by logging their home movie screens on to the website and at first this had been quite popular but after a month, most people had become bored with the slow meticulous progress and lack of interesting finds. So, there were few spectators when, forty days into the dig, the scientists, carefully brushing through a layer of dark carbonised material in the second cave, came upon the first bones. Seven days later, watched avidly by almost the entire population of Gibraltar and probably many thousands around the world, a complete skeleton in remarkably good state of preservation was finally exposed. Although undoubtedly very ancient, hopes that it might be the longed-for

Neanderthal were soon dashed by the experts on site. The prominent eyebrow ridges and the receding chin and forehead, hallmarks of the Neanderthals were missing. Initial examinations revealed a number of interesting facts though and these were eventually released to the public. The skeleton was of a young female and at the time of death she appeared to have been in an advanced stage of pregnancy. What is more, the body seemed to have been covered with some sort of vegetation. Final confirmation of this and the dating of the finds would have to await the full report from England. The skeleton itself together with all data, photos, soil samples, etc. had already been dispatched. It was to be the only find of any significance discovered in these caves

Summary of

Report on human remains found at Gibraltar on 14th September 2200

Location

Small limestone cave situated 126 metres above present beach level.

Description

148 cms complete female skeleton - preservation good.
30 cms complete male skeleton - preservation poor.

Species

Homo sapiens sapiens

Dating

Carbon 14 /Accelerator Mass Spectrometry 4950/5000yrs BP.

Age

Female : 14–16 years / Male: days

DNA

Both skeletons are of very closely related humans.

Position
In situ female supine with child lying on top.

Cause of death
Not obvious – no detectable signs of injuries.

Vegetation surrounding bodies
From pollen analysis and few seeds found, this would appear to be mostly N. papyraceus (Paper White Narcissus) a small plant species once common in the Mediterranean region. It flowers at present during January and February. Its small sweet-scented white flowers covered much of the Rock of Gibraltar in winter, although it is much rarer now.

Conclusion
Possible ritualistic burial of members of Celtiberian peoples which were inhabiting neighbouring areas in southern Spain at this time.

It is unlikely that we will ever know who this young girl holding what appears to be a newborn baby was, whether the child was really hers, (though this seems probable from the DNA results), how she died or how she came to be buried up there in that remote cave and, most intriguing of all, what the purpose of covering her and the baby with the white narcissus was.

The Millennium

33

3000 AD

Today I am one hundred and twenty five years old and have climbed to the top of the old Rock – hardly anyone ever does now unless they are coming to the Terminus. It is a perfect day, they nearly always are. The rains are programmed for the early hours of the mornings. Below me, the sprawling city slumbers on, exhausted after the hectic millennium celebrations last night, that's the trouble with these satellite-lit nights, they go on forever. My heart thumps, but I am not really tired. This is my third heart now, put in two years ago. I shudder at the thought of what people had to go through when they used animal hearts. I don't think I could have done that. Now they are produced from our own stem cells. I have also had gene therapy twice to eliminate alien growths.

As I sit here, I try counting all the things I have had changed. I now have a full head of jet-black hair implanted last year. I decided to go for this colour this time as I was tired of the brown; I even tried blonde once in my youth. I changed my eyes to blue then for a while. Other than the usual changes of teeth, blood vessels, eye lenses, face-lifts and skin rejuvenations, I have only had one kidney regrown. My second wife, Rosie, had a whole arm regrown after the accident. Our son who was with her at the time had to have both his legs done, but they have never been entirely satisfactory. Fortunately our daughter had stayed at home that day. Nearly everyone who wants children now has a son and daughter, it is the maximum permitted. If you have only one child, or better still none at all, you are given large tax allowances.

Despite all this well-being, I am tired of life. I am now due for my biannual check up, but have decided to skip it. I have done everything and seen everything I really want to. I have been on those exhilarating bouncing lunar holidays where the low gravity allows you to really enjoy yourself with minimal effort and even spent a while on Mars. I am seriously thinking of applying for termination. If you do, your dependants are given big tax concessions. My present wife Jean wants to live on though. She is still hoping for great-grandchildren despite the fact that her three grandchildren maintain that they will do without children themselves. All youngsters are now being brainwashed and enticed with huge bribes to opt for sterilisation in an effort to curb the population growth.

I could apply for cloning, but it is difficult to get accepted onto the restricted program and in any case, although many think this to be a form of rejuvenation, I firmly believe that it is the accumulation of experiences and memories as one grows up that really makes the person. I have met the clones of people I knew well and apart from their physical appearance they are quite different.

Below me, at the head of the bay I can see the old tunnel entrances. These are no longer used to cross the Strait as we have the two continuous movement bridges which you sit on to be whisked over to visit the wild life parks on the other side, the only large bit of greenery now visible from the Rock. It is wonderful to see the perfect collection of animals and plants, including many extinct species that have been regenerated from their DNA or in fact have had their DNA reconstructed.

The Rock itself is now practically landlocked except for the southern end. Below me, between the many buildings, I can just about make out the ancient sea walls and further out the faint outlines of what they say were once the moles of a magnificent harbour, all relics of a time when this Rock was almost entirely surrounded by the sea and was a great fortress. This was during the wars of the first and second millennium and the first half of the third before the world order was finally established. The causes of most of these wars were the different nationalities which divided the people as the world then was made up of many countries. Now of course all of this has finished and practically everyone even speaks the same language. Yet I have read that here, within this then small town of Gibraltar, there was a great mix of those nationalities, Genoese, English, Spanish, Portuguese, Moroccans and many others and they all apparently lived in peace and harmony.

The world order that put an end to all the troubles was no doubt accelerated by the detection of alien messages from outer space, undeniable confirmation that we are not alone. Mind you, no one has been able to decipher these yet.

Stretching eastwards into the Mediterranean and far beyond the lands festooned with high-rise buildings, I can just make out the odd flurry on the smooth sea as hundreds of dolphins break the surface pursuing the teeming bait shoals. You can go fishing now and are guaranteed of a bumper catch of prize fish. I wonder what it was like in the days when one reads that fish were difficult to catch. What a thrill it must have been when you did catch one. In any case the biological management of the sea has at long last been achieved and the seas are now the major source of food supply for the planet.

Everything is too perfect now. Everyone is tall, healthy and lean. The food is exquisite, the pleasure drugs delightful and harmless. After so many years of this, I am just plain bored, there is nothing else to see or do. Slowly I get up and ascend the short flight of steps to the Terminus building.

High Tide

34

500,000 ??

Perhaps the most uncanny thing is the overwhelming silence, only the whispering of the wind as it sweeps over the giant sand dunes which come rolling in from the coasts like mighty yellow waves breaks this stillness. All along this drab and fragmented coast the shoreline is dotted with islets and long serpentine fingers of grey water penetrate deep into valleys bereft of all vegetation. To the south, a line of serrated limestone peaks, bleached by the sun, rise from the dark sea. This is all that can be seen of the mighty Rock that once stood here. Now its base and sloping flanks, seared with the relics of past civilisations, lie deep under the waters. Above the tide lines no sign of these remain. Even the peaks that are still visible rising from the sea are frequently engulfed in the frothing giant waves that are often whipped up by the numerous and fearful storms that ravage the great expanses of water.

Across the wide stretch of sea that now separates these two great land masses another line of islands can be seen with a massive domed one in its midst. This last is the remnant of that other great mount that, together with the limestone peak on this side, had stood for ages like two mighty pillars guarding the then narrow Strait. Behind it the purple mountains rise in ranks, seemingly marching into the dry and distant interior. In all a bleak, sterile and forbidding landscape, even the surface of the seas, playground to plesiosaurs, ichthyosaurs, dolphins, whales and many others over the millennia, is now quiescent.

Where now the mighty battles for survival? The ousting and annihilating of whole species in the constant struggles for supremacy. The feeding of one upon the other. The great contenders and ostensibly periodic victors in these ruthless contests, like the giant dinosaurs and clever primates, are long gone. The vast civilisations created by the latter species that straddled and scarred the earth and in the process eliminated so many others to make way for themselves, are vanished.

Now only the wind blows and night follows day inexorably as it did in the beginning, but there is no one, man or beast or grass or tree, to react to this anymore. The land is barren. In the sea though, on rare, calm and moonless nights, minute pinpoints of fluorescence may be seen rising up from the dark and lapping at the base of the old limestone Rock. Are these the residues of some deep watery chemical reactions or could it be that life is stirring in the abyss again?

The Closing of the Gates

35

1,000,000 ??

Report

Location:	Star 2489/GFX
Operation:	Investigation of second relic radio/sonar pulse detected on 3rd planet out.
Site :	White rock on edge of rift between two of the largest tectonic plates on this planet.

Landed at first light by one of two large mounds (Composition: compressed fragmented remains of minute calcite life forms). Separated by a narrow gorge through which a small stream flows into a broad depression beyond. The pulse to be investigated emanates from deep inside this rock mound that bears vestiges of habitation by the bipedal life form (Intelligence Quota 3xb) which dominated the planet before this galaxy passed through the Quadrix Radiation Belt. This radiation eliminated them, together with all life forms on this planet as well as the colonies they had established on its single satellite and on the 4th planet out. The pulse mechanism was finally located sealed deep below the base of this white mound and rebounds off the top of the adjoining one. Whilst the mechanism for emitting this pulse is relatively primitive, the automatic driving force is ingenious and uses the radiant heat of the star reflecting on the white surface of the mound, hence its longevity. A similar system has already been found and neutralised on this planet's satellite.

Observation

This rock, which has been subjected to extensive tilting over the aeons since it was first thrust up, has undergone further movement after the installation of the pulsar system. Both of these rocky outcrops were higher at that time before eroding to their present forms. They were much further apart and separated by a very large river or other wide body of water. It is theorised that the pulse originally shot across underwater and rebounded off the base of the adjoining mountain.

Function

Probably military, presumably for controlling the passage through this strait – the dominant animals here at the time of extinction are known to have been highly aggressive.

Conclusion

Within the next millennia the remnants of these two mounds, which have been eroding and converging since their creation, will be crushed together as the two massive plates, whose momentum originally caused their elevation, continue to flow towards each other and eventually meet.

Note

Small areas of blue and green algae detected on mound's rock surfaces denoting the resurgence of life forms on this planet.

Action

Pulsar Mechanism deactivated.

Relic sonar and radio signals investigation report by Inter-Galactic Flight GT764Z

Djebel Al-Fath

The ships came to the mountain of double victory
Whose venerated heights are the most famous of all mountains
Clouds form an unbuttoned black cloak round the neck of its superb
summit
Stars crown the air above it like dinars of gold
And their golden rays caress it.
This ancient mountain has blunted its teeth in the
Forests of time and the passage of centuries.
Wise in experience, it has known all manner of things
Has shaken off all vicissitudes and pushed them away
Like the camel drivers jostle their camels
And continue on the road singing glad songs.
The mountain is now at rest and ponders
On its past, its present, and its future
In grave and thoughtful silence, hiding many mysteries.
May this Rock be secure as from tomorrow
Safe from fear and misfortune
Although all other mountains in the world tremble!

Abu Abdallah ibn Ghalib Arrossafy's panegyric of the
Caliph Abd al-Mumin, 1162 AD.

As adapted by Tito Benady.

Bibliography

A History of the Late Siege of Gibraltar, 1785, J. Drinkwater, T. Spilsbury, London.

A la Sombra de la Roca, A. Escuadra, 1997, Ayuntamiento de La Linea, Cordoba.

Civil Hospital and Epidemics in Gibraltar, S. Benady, 1994, Gibraltar Books, Grendon.

The Fortress Came First, T. J. Finlayson, 1991, Gibraltar Books, Grendon.

'The Founding of Gibraltar', T. Benady, 1994, *Gibraltar Heritage Journal,* No 2.

Gibraltar at the End of the Millenium, C. and G. Finlayson, 1999, Aquila Services, Gibraltar.

'Gibraltar During the Spanish Civil War', I. Benyunes, *Gibraltar Heritage Journal,* No 2.

Gibraltar, The Making of a People, Dr J. J. Garcia, 1994, Medsun, Gibraltar.

History of the British Colonies: Possessions in Europe, R. Montgomerie Martin, 1835, London.

The History of Gibraltar, H. Chichon, 1981, Teacher's Centre, Gibraltar.

La Compra de Gibraltar por los Conversos Andaluces, D. Lamelas, 1976, Madrid.

Mediaeval Gibraltar, J. J. Alcantara, 1979, Medsun, Gibraltar.

The Rock of the Gibraltarians, Sir William G.F. Jackson, 1987, Associated University Presses, USA.

The Story of Gibraltar, H. W. Howes, 1946, Philip & Tacey, London.

The Streets of Gibraltar, T. Benady, 1996, Gibraltar Books, Grendon.

Travels in Asia and Africa 1325 – 1354, Ibn Battuta, 1929, Routledge and Kegan Paul, London.

'Voyages of Ibn Batoutah', C. Defremery and B. R. Sanguinetti, *Gibraltar Heritage Journal,* No 2.